LOVE JII

Mihir Srivastava is a Delhi-based journalist with an interest in painting. A senior associate editor with the weekly newspaper *Patriot*, he has previously worked with leading news magazines such as *India Today*, *Outlook* and *Tehelka* over the last fifteen years. An existentialist, he likes to visit people instead of places and backpacks every year in Europe and other parts of the world. For him, travelling is not simply a pleasure. It is serious business.

Raul Irani is the photo editor of *Open* magazine. Inspired by his father, a journalist, he started work as a photojournalist at the age of fifteen, using a digital camera his parents had bought him after selling the family jewellery. He is known for his affability and humour, loves Sufi music and is an undiscovered cricket prodigy with the unique distinction of hitting six sixes in one over at a university-level cricket match.

Love Jihadis

AN OPEN-MINDED JOURNEY
INTO THE HEART OF
WESTERN UTTAR PRADESH

MIHIR SRIVASTAVA
RAUL IRANI

First published by Westland Publications Private Limited in 2020

1st Floor, A Block, East Wing, Plot No. 40, SP Infocity, Dr MGR Salai, Perungudi, Kandanchavadi, Chennai 600096

Westland and the Westland logo are the trademarks of Westland Publications Private Limited, or its affiliates.

Copyright © Mihir Srivastava and Raul Irani, 2020
Photographs copyright © Raul Irani, 2020

ISBN: 9789389152326

10 9 8 7 6 5 4 3 2 1

Typeset by SŪRYA, New Delhi

Printed at Replika Press Pvt. Ltd.

CONTENTS

TO MAMU, WHO IS NO LONGER WITH US

People call him Mamu. In his mid-thirties, he looks older than he ought to. A local news photographer—a good one—he drinks more alcohol than his body can handle. Journalists in Meerut know him well; he has been around for a good fifteen years, shooting photographs as part of his day job. Mamu is our local contact in Meerut, helpfully connecting us with people and opening doors for us in and around Meerut.

Tall and lanky, the muscles have melted off his broad frame. He must have been a hunk once. Recently, he began drinking countrymade liquor because a doctor advised that it's less harmful than whisky. There's an element of pride in this addiction: he drinks his own liquor. His friends have stopped judging him. He doesn't contest their views. He can be a boaster, an emotional fool, very helpful, in need of love, but his drinking habit repels people.

A strong life force propels Mamu day in and day out, even though his liver is damaged. He has been admitted to the hospital a few times, and let off each time with a stern warning that he must mend his ways. His job is not inspiring; it doesn't even pay enough for his addiction. He gets a paltry five hundred rupees for every photograph that is published. Money is a problem, but he has the support of a fairly accommodating family. His mother hopes that things will change. He's grateful, but not strong enough to make the change.

Mamu is usually drunk, but he functions perfectly through it. To lead a life while inebriated is a skill. He rides his bike at a constant, if slow, speed, unperturbed, apparently in no hurry to get anywhere. I rode pillion with him a few times and felt safe. This is not to suggest that I'm encouraging drunk-driving, of course.

One of the things Mamu loves doing is feeding his friends—I'm very grateful to him—but he hardly ever eats anything himself. He has odd, yet fixed, timings for his frugal meals. He introduced us to some exciting local cuisine.

Lack of proper employment is probably worse than being unemployed. Mamu is desperate for money and money makes him desperate. He finds innovative ways to make a quick buck, such as helping friends get things done at local government offices in return for cash or some other consideration. He is not a mercenary; he is a kind-hearted man struggling with a crisis of his own making. There are people he loves, people who know he loves them, but none of this is expressed in words. He rarely gets a heartfelt conversation.

～

He died a few months ago. This book is our gift to his memory. Thank you, Mamu.

AN INTRODUCTORY NOTE

Hindus and Muslims have coexisted in India for centuries, their lives integrally linked. There is a term for the composite culture they have developed: Ganga–Jamuni tehzeeb. Though there have been flashpoints of discord in the past, in hindsight, those clashes seem like some sort of an adjustment process—a show of relative strength and then a reaffirmation of the fact that peaceful coexistence is the only viable option for mutual survival.

Western Uttar Pradesh has always been communally sensitive, especially in cities like Aligarh, Meerut, Agra and Bulandshahr. There have always been hardliners among both Hindus and Muslims, believers of the philosophy of 'the clash of civilisations', who advocate that the propagation of their faith essentially entails the annihilation of other faiths. The problem has been compounded by the political patronage these elements enjoy. The demolition of the Babri Masjid in 1992 by militant Hindu organisations, claiming that the mosque had been built on what had previously been the temple of Lord Rama, was a turning point. While the right-wing Bharatiya Janata Party, together with militant Hindu organisations like the Vishwa Hindu

Parishad, was held responsible for the demolition of the mosque, the Congress party that ruled at the Centre and failed to stop the destruction was equally responsible. A monster was thus unleashed that is now difficult to contain.

Political fortunes changed due to this one dastardly crime. Stoking communal passions became a legitimate way to garner votes, leading to a society polarised on religious lines. In the past six years, there have been clashes for reasons more political than social.

In 2014, a love jihad case in Meerut made 'love' a sinister ploy to undermine faith. In 2015, fifty-year-old Mohammad Akhlaq was lynched to death by an unruly mob on the mere suspicion that he was storing beef. Akhlaq's son, twenty-two-year-old Danish, sustained serious injuries in the attack, but survived. There were contradictory reports about the meat procured from Akhlaq's house. One report claimed it was goat meat while others said it was indeed beef. Cow vigilantes or gau-rakshaks have killed an estimated forty-four people in the last five years.

Then, there were reports in December 2014 about a group of Muslim ragpickers who had converted to Hinduism in a phenomenon that was dubbed 'ghar vapsi' or homecoming. Last but not the least, it was alleged that many 'Hindu' families migrated out of the small Muslim-majority town of Kairana between 2014 and 2016 due to threats from a mafia organisation led by a Muslim. It was alleged that this 'exodus' was akin to what had happened to the Pandits in the Kashmir valley nearly three decades ago.

Most of these cases turned out to be political hoaxes that a subservient mainstream media played on the people of India. After the elections, most of these cases were no longer pursued. The accused, portrayed as sinister villains, were the real victims, their lives destroyed. Their story is that of grit and determination in the face of insurmountable odds.

We visited some of these people after the dust had settled. The suspicion between the two communities has become stronger; the mistrust that had been fanned to garner votes has had a lasting impact.

How easy is it to fool people? This book confirms the obvious: that politicians are skilled at it, and social media and technology make it only easier for them.

But our travels also showed us that the forces that bind Hindus and Muslims are stronger than mistrust and suspicion.

~

Raul Irani and I are journalists and friends. We were colleagues at a news organisation and got to know each other well enough to decide to do a book together.

Love jihad is an issue close to our hearts. How can any state tell its subjects who to marry and who not to? Adults have the right to choose their spouses. But what is happening in India now goes beyond directives on who not to marry. 'We the people' are told what to eat and what not to eat, what to wear and what not to wear, and are lectured daily on culture, morality and ethics. Goons routinely police the day-to-day lives of common people. They are violent people who lynch innocents with impunity.

This book, however, is not an investigation. It's merely a travelogue by two disgruntled journalists. Generally feeling under-utilised, we decided to visit places in western Uttar Pradesh that had recently been in the news for communal issues. Only disgruntled journalists visit such places.

But we felt the need to make this journey through the Hindi heartland where all communal discord seems to originate. This area continues to remain potentially volatile. Love jihad originated in these fertile plains; so did cow vigilantism, and ghar vapsi. Over a year, Raul and I spent weekends in cities like Meerut, Muzaffarnagar, Aligarh, Hapur and Mathura. On two occasions, we stayed longer than a week.

This is a simple narrative of people, places and things anyone would encounter if they cared to visit. It is ironic that, despite the intense media attention that western UP received when communal issues flared up, many crucial facts still remain broadly unreported. To us, every bit of it was a revelation, including the fact that it was so accessible.

That brings us to the question of how information is disseminated in India. This is an emotional issue for both Raul and I. Any journalist who is proud of the power of the written word has reason to be disillusioned. A report should reflect reality, not obfuscate it. But there are substantive reasons to believe that 'journalism' today is not being practised in its true spirit. There are powerful extraneous considerations at play, which Indian journalists have had to learn to live with. Some of us have given in to these pressures and have made a fortune; others, who haven't, are languishing in the margins.

While this is not a book about media ethics, the lack of it is certainly what motivated us to travel through western UP and see for ourselves what is really happening there.

And when you do that, when you share the other side of the story, amplify the voices of people who fall under the broad category of 'dispensable', their lives merely a means to a certain end, you distil the distinction between journalism and propaganda.

In a battle of perception, facts are malleable. We all have our biases, and that includes the media. But if the media deliberately misleads people, it's a problem.

Love jihad is actually a non-issue. But it has been made an issue, inserted into the popular psyche by the concerted efforts of pliant media houses. The reality on the ground is nothing like that.

For instance, take Sanauallah of Sarawaha village in Meerut district, anointed 'mastermind of love jihad' and charged with gang-raping Shallu, a Hindu girl who had dared to marry a Muslim boy, together with Kalim, her husband. This heinous charge against Sanauallah was the figment of someone's imagination, because Shallu confessed that she had been forced by her own family on threat of death to file an FIR against Sanauallah and four other people. Her family seemingly had the support of the state.

Sanauallah is a tragic figure in this story, but the tragedy is laced with some irony. He and his wife were jailed for more than a year and their children suffered immensely. Sanauallah was the face of 'love jihad', broadcast live on every television screen in the country. Now that the elections are over and people like him have served their purpose in the politics of communal vote banks, no one talks about them. No one bothers to investigate whether the 'mastermind' is alive or dead, in jail or out on bail.

Sanauallah is a victim of an injustice perpetrated at the behest of the state. And now, he finds it difficult to bear how he has been summarily ignored since his release from jail. He misses the media attention, even though it spelled doom for him. He wants to be heard again. This time, with his version of events, what he went through, how he feels about his country. But no one is interested. So, we lent him an ear.

It's only a coincidence that Raul and I are from different communities. I'm a Hindu who supports no particular political outfit. Raul is a Muslim; a liberal man with an artistic bent of mind. Raul harbours a latent anger, I feel. It's increasingly difficult to be a Muslim in India. The minorities of the country are facing an existential crisis. They are constantly reminded that they're different and despised for those differences, and they routinely have to prove their love and loyalty for the nation.

Raul's father is a journalist and his brother, a teacher. They want to live in peace. When we were out reporting, his father would phone us every few hours to enquire about our welfare. He wasn't keen on having his son involved in a project that could stir up a hornet's nest.

Raul's father's attitude is typical of most Muslim elders. For them, survival means having the wisdom to go about their business while being careful not to offend anyone, and hope for a better time when they won't be judged because of their faith. People from minority communities are afraid. Those in power should be worried about this but they take it as a compliment.

And let's be clear about this: Muslims, relegated to the position of second-grade citizens, don't feel safe. To ensure safety, the elders want their young folk to lie low, attract no undue attention and act as if nothing has happened when faced with an aggravation. Young blood is not so easily cooled. Younger Muslims want to resist. They seek dignity. Usually, though, the elders prevail. When they are united, Hindus and Muslims make a great team. I like to think this book is another example of what can be achieved when the two communities work together—even if it may seem simplistic. We enjoyed our various trips to western UP, even the encounters with people who appeared to be living in denial and had fixed ideas about how things are and how they should be. To avoid any possible lack of trust, we didn't always identify ourselves by our real names. Raul became 'Rahul' when we visited militant Hindu organisations. I became 'Mir', instead of Mihir, when we met representatives of the orthodox Muslim community. As they say, '*Naam mein kya rakha hai* (what's in a name)?'

In this partnership, I have done most of the text, while Raul took all the photographs. Pictures are important, for they are a stark representation of reality. They tell an irrefutable story and also substantiate the text. We wanted visual validation of what we have written as a service to people who look the other way when a narrative is not in consonance with their world view. We wanted our readers to be co-travellers in this journey.

Working on this book was a serious endeavour, but Raul and I also had a great deal of fun, eating out at dhabas, trying local cuisines, enjoying pleasant winter nights.

We were travellers in our own homeland, trying to make sense of what it had become. What we learned is that despite the negativity, not all is lost. The composite culture of India is intact and fairly robust, at least in this region. What is happening in the country now will pass.

SARAWAHA

SHALLU

In the village of Sarawaha in Meerut, eighteen-year-old Shallu Tyagi wanted a job. The bright and lively college student knew that earning a living would give her the freedom to make her own choices. For young women in this part of the country, however, freedom is an untested thing, a quirky fantasy that is rarely realised. Shallu discovered this the hard way.

She wanted to work, to buy a mobile phone, have friends, and not be confined to the four walls of her home, making food, feeding cattle and doing the mundane activities that consumed her mother's and grandmother's lives. So, in late 2013, she joined a local primary school as a teacher for a salary of five hundred rupees a month, which she used as pocket money.

Rural western Uttar Pradesh is deeply, nakedly patriarchal. Attitudes are changing now, but at a snail's pace. '*Ladki hasi, mane fasi* (if a girl smiles back at you, she's ready to sleep with you)' is how men perceive women in a severely gender-segregated society. The purdah system is prevalent among both Hindus and Muslims, though the latter are more rigorous about it. Women, it is believed, need to be hidden away, like family jewels.

But these days, educated girls—graduates, to be precise—don't cover their faces after puberty. That's the privilege of a degree: even men are awed. They roam around freely on their bicycles and, despite family resistance and the misgivings of mostly older women and younger brothers, even do odd jobs to make some money. They want smartphones and will save for months to buy one that allows selfies and a connection to the internet, specifically the encrypted messaging app WhatsApp. For these women confined to the dark, dank areas of their homes, WhatsApp is a window to the world. They can take pictures of themselves, talk and create their own little space in the outside world. Technology and education have become potent tools against repression and segregation.

Shallu was a confident young woman. She was open to new experiences, had lots of friends and liked to be outdoors. And if necessary, she was prepared to defy the diktats of the male members of her extended family, some even younger than her, who would try and repress her spirit. She was not averse to talking to men outside her family. That is not a crime, but in this patriarchal society, it is treated like one. In her late teens and very early twenties, Shallu had the economic independence to do as she liked.

But she had no idea that, in the months to come, that very freedom of choice would make her a household name. Because Shallu did the unthinkable. She fell in love with a Muslim man—Kalim—and decided to marry him. That act of choice unleashed the wrath not only of her family, but also of the political and religious establishments of India.

She·was held captive by her own family who threatened her life, and had to run away and live for a year in a government facility for destitute women simply to survive. Her husband and four other people—unknown to her—were charged with and jailed for abducting and gang-raping her. She had to cope with becoming the symbol of 'love jihad'—a term coined by innovative propagandists in the media and the establishment to politicise the love between Hindus and Muslims.

Over the next year or so, Shallu would need to demonstrate the strength of her belief in her independence. She would have to do this publicly, facing both a highly opinionated and judgmental political and religious population, and the courts of India.

The next few pages are an account of Shallu's tryst with destiny, based on her depositions to the district court in Meerut and the Allahabad High Court, as she battled for her basic freedom to function as an independent adult.

~

In late 2013, Shallu began work as a teacher at a school run by her tau (father's older brother) for a paltry monthly salary of five hundred rupees, or eight US dollars a month. However, she signed a payslip for seven hundred rupees. The two hundred rupees she did not receive probably went to her tau as his cut for persuading the family to allow her to work. Exploitation, like charity, begins at home.

A few months later, a madrassa in Sarawaha advertised for an English teacher and offered a salary of two thousand rupees a month. Shallu was interested. Why shouldn't she be? All right, it was a madrassa—a Muslim school—

but the pay offered was four times her current salary. And she wouldn't be required to hand over a part of it to her employers—there were no hidden costs. It made economic sense to apply for the job, and so, Shallu joined the madrassa as an English teacher. She worked there for eight months.

We visited the madrassa in Sarawaha on a sunny December afternoon in 2017. It is located right opposite an old temple—the biggest in the region—which reminded me of the Nagara temple architecture I had studied in school. The temple and the madrassa are separated by a recently constructed brick-lined road. The fruits of development are finally trickling down, at least to this village. It is possible to drive through the narrow brick roads of the village, though there are many tight corners. A wide drain runs along the road outside the high, white-painted walls of the madrassa.

The gates of the madrassa are hinged to tall pillars that join to form an arch covered with flower-patterned tiles. The entrance is so fine that one imagines the madrassa would be huge, but that is not the case. To the right of a rectangular plot of land about an acre in size, there is a small structure consisting of three or four rooms in a row, all opening into a common elongated veranda that is also used for classes. A tall tree stands at the far end, beneath which the children often play cricket after school. Not a blade of grass is to be seen; the loose mud baking in the sun makes for a soft dusty floor. On the left, along the periphery, there are two covered toilets.

This is a special madrassa that provides modern education along with the regular curriculum of the scriptures and Quran. It is special also because it teaches its students—children aged between three and fifteen—four languages: Hindi, English, Urdu and Arabic. This alone would humble many public schools in Delhi. Raul and I were welcomed to the school, and soon discovered that many of the teachers were in their late teens. These young teachers were the strictest of all the members of the staff, never hesitating to use their rulers on troublemakers. Like an inspector of schools, I visited each of the classrooms and interacted with the pupils. To confirm that they could read English, I asked them to read from their textbooks. They could, and the girls did much better than the boys. They were fluent and read with immaculate pronunciation. 'The revolution of knowledge begins in classrooms like this one,' I told the pupils, impressed by the efforts of teachers like Shallu. (She had quit four years ago.)

I chatted with Iqbal, one of the students at the madrassa. He was a class IX pupil of a local English medium school, but he attended the madrassa too, to study the Quran and scriptures. A tall, skinny boy with an expressive face and intent eyes, Iqbal insisted on conversing with me in English. He needs English to travel and explore the world, he told me, so he must constantly find opportunities to practice speaking the language. 'English will help me connect with foreigners,' he said. 'I'm happy and grateful to you for speaking with me in English.' He shook hands like a politician, gripping mine between both of his own.

It was fun hanging out with the children. They have so much energy and enthusiasm, so much curiosity about everything new—Raul and I kept them excited. Watching them repeat Quranic verses over and over, I mused about how early they are initiated into the tenets of their faith. The smaller children, aged below five, were particularly entertaining. They sat with folded legs on rows of mats in the open and bent forward slightly while chorusing their lessons aloud. Each class of about thirty students was separated from the others by a gap in the rows, and keeping these nearly three hundred restless children seated while they learned their verses by recitation, was obviously quite a tedious task for their teachers. I felt I had entered a poultry farm with hundreds of birds in cages.

The teachers were busy, shouting at the students collectively and individually. The legs of the pupils were restless, aching to run. Dust acted like a cushion on the ground.

For the first three years of schooling, we were told, pupils would just shift towards the right as they were promoted to higher classes. There are no blackboards for the junior classes; the mode of instruction is oral.

From class V onwards, pupils have covered classrooms complete with blackboards. However, there are no desks and chairs. They still sit on dusty mats on the floor to study.

Our presence at the madrassa disrupted the day's routine. The children were excited to see us. Raul, with his big cameras, was like a celebrity from an alien world. He took pictures while I talked to the teachers. Most of them were new; even the principal had joined only a few months earlier. None of them had met Shallu.

'Will we be on television?' asked a young student who couldn't contain his curiosity. Risking admonition, he had interrupted my conversation with the teachers. 'I have a new television at home.'

'One day you will be on television,' I assured the boy. Listening to them chant their lessons later, when the excitement had died and the boys and girls had settled down to study, I suddenly knew what this madrassa reminded me of. The constant murmur of all those recitations sounded like the simultaneous purring of a thousand cats. A symphony of cats! The image made me smile, even as I tried to decipher the language they were using. Was it Hindi, English, Urdu or Arabic? Does the language of the land have any bearing to the way cats purr, I wondered. Do cats purr differently in, say, Germany as compared to France or England?

As my thoughts drifted off, Raul continued to shoot pictures frantically, wielding his camera like a machine gun. The comparison made sense. After all, this madrassa had been described by the local newspapers as 'a terror factory'. And Shallu had been working here when she met her future husband, Kalim.

Perhaps, the madrassa's brush with notoriety had made the teachers cautious. While the children posed happily for Raul's camera, the younger teachers slipped behind pillars and trees. Cameras, after all, can bring trouble. The images they shoot can one day make you the face of controversy.

When I'm not talking, I like shooting pictures of Raul at work. At the madrassa, we felt as if we were a part of the whole experience. In fact, it felt like a family affair.

For young children, a madrassa is a much-needed outing from their cramped homes. Away from protective parents, they have the opportunity to meet and interact with others their age. For the first time in their lives, they are disciplined to behave as a cohesive group that adheres to a common faith. To some, this happened naturally. Others struggled.

Though it is despised as 'rote learning', the oral mode of instruction serves a purpose. Memorising scriptures by way of endless repetitions, their bodies rocking back and forth in sync with the rhythm, helps children internalise what they are learning. Before they realise it, these scriptures are ingrained in their psyches. Since this happens so early in their life, the scripture in a way shapes them, and guides them for the rest of their lives. Watching it happen was heart-warming.

I saw no signs of 'terror' in the school. Certainly not the skinny maulvi in his late teens with a bony face, big, serious eyes, a dense, curly beard on the conical chin of his thin face, wielding a too-ready ruler in his desperation to assert his authority over the senior Quran class that had students only a few years younger than him. 'Where's the bomb factory?' I asked a teacher. He wasn't amused.

This madrassa, a place of Islamic learning for beginners, with such an emphasis on modern education that it even employed a Hindu teacher like Shallu, had been described in various papers as a hotbed of terror activities. How? Why?

Was it because Shallu found herself attracted to Islam, something her family could not fathom? In her bayaan (deposition), handwritten in Hindi, dated 11 July 2016, Shallu stated: 'Muslim religion was being taught [at the madrassa] and I liked it.' She was forthright: 'I was attracted to Islam.' Her emphasis was on the word 'I'. She even told

Pooja, a friend of hers, that she liked the Muslim religion. 'But if I become a Muslim, who will marry me?' she asked her friend. This was in early 2014.

The question of marriage is integral to the life of a woman in any Indian village. Any attraction, infatuation or romance is expected to lead to matrimony, as if it is a crime to be single and open to mingling. At the same time, courtship without the explicit consent of the family is blasphemous.

Shallu felt the need for a man in her life as both a friend and a lover. Pooja encouraged her to meet a Muslim man by the name of Kalim. When Shallu and Kalim met, they liked each other enough for Pooja to tell Shallu, 'He's the kind of man who'd marry you [even though you are a Hindu].'

Kalim is a petty trader who makes and sells paneer (cottage cheese). He is the oldest of four brothers and two sisters. Shallu and he met and they bonded, and chatted regularly on the phone. Then, they started meeting each other whenever the opportunity arose. Their feelings for each grew stronger, and it wasn't long before they started what their urban counterparts call 'dating.' And then, they became intimate.

All was well till Shallu realised she was pregnant. There was no way they could have this child. Neither of them was ready to confront the world with their relationship. They didn't know what to do.

Their confusion ended when a complication arose. Shallu needed immediate medical attention when she began feeling severe pain. She and Kalim went to the medical college in Meerut for treatment, posing as a married couple.

The foetus, they were told, was growing in Shallu's fallopian tube rather than in her uterus. On the advice of the doctor, the child was aborted on 27 July 2014. Shallu remained in the hospital for the next three days.

Her long absence was unexplained and her family grew anxious. When she returned to her home in Sarawaha, Shallu explained what had happened, telling them the whole story. It was a brave thing to do.

In return for the truth, Shallu was beaten up by the members of her family. This was both a punishment for breaking society's rules, and a warning to never do such a thing again.

But Shallu had had a taste of independence. She was not going to let it go so easily. Defiant and afraid for her life, she slipped out the next morning on the pretext of visiting a friend (she refused to identify this friend in her deposition later), took a bus to the neighbouring town of Hapur, about an hour away from Sarawaha, and stayed with a friend whom, again, she refused to identify in her deposition. (Later, in her testimony to the Allahabad High Court in 2016, she said this friend was Pooja.)

Shallu was now on her own, and traumatised by the assault on her life by her own family. It took her a few days to calm down enough to be able to think about the future; to understand the implications and consequences of her bold decision.

She was aware that her family would be looking for her, so she remained in hiding. After a few days, she mustered up enough courage to step out and try to look for Kalim at Arya Kanya College in Hapur. Instead, she found members of her extended family, along with a neighbour, Nirakar

Tyagi. They had stationed themselves at the college, hoping to find her.

Her involvement with a Muslim man was blasphemous, they told her. According to Shallu's statement, on 2 August 2014, she was forced into a car and transported to Kailli, a village not very far from Hapur where some of her relatives lived.

Every member of Shallu's extended family felt obliged to safeguard the family's honour. In the north of India, the 'honour of the family' is often about the control of women's bodies and the stamping out of their desires. All those able-bodied men in Shallu's family felt emasculated by her defiance. In their eyes, she was a threat to the good reputation of their village, their traditions and their culture.

Her love for a Muslim man could not be justified. She was not capable of making a decision like this, they said. They reasoned that she had been manipulated and indoctrinated to do what she did. She couldn't have understood what she was doing. And she had been blinded by desire. Because of this, Shallu had to be kept in confinement. And they were more than willing to use force to 'persuade' her.

Her family wanted answers. Where had she been for the last few days? They wanted her to lead them to Kalim. She didn't say a word despite the pressure.

The men of the family huddled in a closed-door conference to decide their course of action. It is clear that they allowed their imagination free flight, because they came up with a plan that would declare Kalim and four others as conspirators, kidnappers and rapists, and Shallu as the victim.

After that, according to Shallu's testimony, she was taken to a park in a village called Kuldhara where her tau, Narendra Tyagi, arrived. His job was to browbeat Shallu into submission. She was threatened with dire consequences. She'd be killed if she didn't comply, he told her. He even carried a pistol. 'He threatened me to tell where I was for the last few days (sic). To which I said, "Tauji, I'm not wrong. Try to understand me,"' Shallu said.

Because she refused to tell them where she had been, they snatched her sling bag and examined it. There, they found an affidavit.

A cousin Shallu identified as Sachin Tyagi read the affidavit aloud. 'Shallu has converted to Islam,' he informed the family.

Her pleas for mercy only instigated them further. Her family felt that they had the moral right to torture her. One of her relatives pulled out a knife and threatened to kill her. They used that knife to remove the dressing on her abdomen—the dressing that had been placed there after the abortion only a few days earlier.

Then some of them began digging a trench nearby, threatening to bury her alive 'unless I say what they want me to tell the whole world (sic)'. They recorded on video what she was tutored to say. Her life was spared.

Shallu was taken to Kharkhoda police station. The media was informed. Members of the media in turn informed Hindu ultra right-wingers. A large number of belligerent people arrived, including members of the media and local office bearers of the Shiv Sena and Bajrang Dal. When Shallu arrived at the police station, they began railing against Muslims and demanding that the police act on Shallu's scripted complaint. Within seconds, Shallu's personal life became a sensitive communal issue. She was forced to register an FIR against Kalim and four other men for not only abducting her but also gang-raping her. When her father got to the police station a while later, he was made a complainant in the case. He signed without much fuss.

After the police complaint was filed, Shallu was shifted to the mahila thana (women's police station). Because she was in excruciating pain and was feeling giddy, she had to be taken to a local hospital, accompanied by her father, her uncle Devendra Tyagi and his son Sandeep Tyagi, as well as a host of strangers. Suddenly, she had become prized property. After a couple of hours, her condition stablised, and she returned to the mahila thana.

At around 8 p.m., well past sunset, Shallu was sent to a government hospital for another medical check-up, after which she returned to the thana and signed some more paperwork before finally being allowed to return to her village with her family.

Though she had been forced to make the complaint, Shallu had not been entirely quiescent during the day. At the mahila thana, she had tried to impress upon the station officer that she had been assaulted in the park by her relatives and people from her village, that her medical dressing had been pulled off, that she had been forced to file a false complaint and that she needed help because her life was at stake. But her pleas fell on deaf ears.

The next day, 4 August 2014, Shallu was presented before the court. A man stepped on her foot, cutting the skin and making her bleed. He was one of her family's lawyers and had stamped on her feet to convey that she should not speak in court that day. She obediently told the judge that she was not well, so the matter was postponed to another day. The family needed more time to strategise.

Shallu was lodged for the day at the house of a relative in Shastri Nagar, Meerut. The family consulted two lawyers whom she met later when they briefed her on what to tell the judge in court the next morning.

For now, she decided to do as she was told. She had tried to tell the police the truth, but they had accepted her family's version of events instead. In court the next day, Shallu told the magistrate what the lawyers had told her to say.

Two policemen were in the magistrate's chamber where she gave her statement. When the statement was being written out, her father was summoned. He remained seated in the chamber for ten minutes, and then went outside again. 'I don't remember how long my statement was recorded (sic). There was a noise outside, sloganeering and hurling of insults. I was scared,' she recollected later.

'I made this statement under duress,' Shallu said in Hindi in her confession. This is an understatement. Shallu's situation was much worse than the word 'duress' can convey. She'd had a painful pregnancy and an abortion. Then, she was assaulted by her relatives and threatened with death. She had been forced to make a false complaint against her lover, and she had been constantly harangued by her family. Her health deteriorated fast.

Shallu had to be shifted to a hospital. Her family, accompanied by a few police personnel, took her to Yashoda Hospital in Ghaziabad, some forty kilometres from Sarawaha, a two-hour drive. After she recovered, she returned to her parents' home in Kharkhoda's Sarawaha. She stayed there for a week. If her family thought that Shallu had given up, they were wrong. She just needed some time to gain the strength to deal with the biggest challenge life had thrown her way.

Life in the village was not easy. Shallu and her family had become the subject of ridicule among neighbours, friends and villagers. At home, she was frequently slapped by her mother; her father who had initially been sympathetic to her cause, or at least not violent, gave in to the mounting pressure and turned against her. She was completely alone and cornered, and she feared for her life.

She stayed with her parents for a month and a half, and watched politicians arriving to express solidarity with the family as though the Tyagis were soldiers being denied their pensions. One day, a police party visited to make further enquiries. After they left, her father and other members of her family thrashed her. '[They] kicked and punched me,' Shallu wrote in her statement.

The only saving grace was Shallu's grandmother, who disliked the way the family was treating the girl, and told her to escape before she was killed. So, in the dark hours of 12 October 2014, Shallu ran away. She ran through the fields of crops as fast as her legs could carry her, feeling as though death was trailing her in the darkness. The ten kilometres she ran and walked to the nearest mahila thana must have taken her a couple of hours. At the mahila thana, she pleaded to be rescued from her family. They had become the most imminent threat to her life.

She was presented before the city magistrate to narrate her story. On the order of the magistrate, she was admitted to Nari Niketan, a government home for destitute women, where she was to stay for the next thirteen months. In the meantime, Kalim and four others would be arrested and jailed for nearly a year.

Shallu's sole desire was to meet her lover upon her release. She felt detached from her roots and her family. Solitude only affirmed her resolve. After a year or so, she was produced before a bench of the Allahabad High Court. Based on her deposition, the bench concluded that Shallu was a major (over twenty-one years old) and competent to make her own choices. The court ordered the authorities to take her wherever she wanted to go. She went to Kalim. His family took her in as Kalim's wife.

At the Allahabad High Court, Shallu filed a petition to quash the FIR against Kalim in which he and several others were accused of kidnapping and raping her, among other offences. In response, Shallu's brother produced her school-leaving certificate before the court. Since school-leaving certificates mention the holder's date of birth, they are considered birth certificates for all practical purposes. According to this school certificate, Shallu was sixteen years, nine months and twenty days old on 11 August 2014. Given that she was a minor when she met Kalim, she was not competent to decide who to marry, her brother argued. Going by this argument, Kalim and the others named in the FIR, had illegitimately detained his sister, and tortured her physically and mentally.

When she returned to court to face this petition, Shallu—now referred to as Sonia alias Firdaus—told the court that she was a major and had of her own 'free will' walked out of her parental house and entered into matrimony with

Kalim. Justices V.K. Shukla and Arvind Kumar Mishra of the Allahabad High Court did not quash the FIR against Kalim and the others, but they ordered the local magistrate to determine Shallu's age to his satisfaction within a month. The justices also directed Shallu to approach the local senior superintendent of police for protection when she needed to appear before the court or go for a medical examination.

After the age issue was settled in favour of Shallu, she clarified that she was in love with Kalim and that she wanted to stay with him of her own free will. No coercion was involved in her affair with Kalim, she asserted. On the contrary, she had been pressured by her family to falsely state that she had been tricked into the relationship. Further, she wrote in her statement, 'It is wrong to say that as long as I lived with my family, at that time no one assaulted/tortured me (sic). It is wrong to say that I gave my statement out of free will before the magistrate; I was scared. It is wrong to say that I was alone in the room with the magistrate when I made the statement.'

Even the police had supported Shallu's family. Why wouldn't they when the sitting minister of state for foreign affairs, former army chief General V.K. Singh, a member of Parliament from neighbouring Ghaziabad, had been seen sympathising with the family and offering them his support?

In her statement on 11 July 2016, Shallu was asked whether she was aware that a Muslim man can have as many as four wives, and she replied that she was well aware of the fact. She didn't exactly remember when she converted to Islam, she said, but it happened in 2013.

'Today (December 2016), I'm a Muslim, I married Kalim [on] 4 December 2013. I was married in the house of relatives of Kalim. The Shaher Kazi of Meerut solemnised the marriage,' she said.

According to this statement, she had converted to Islam a year before her marriage with Kalim. 'I converted to Islam by filling a shapath patra (affidavit) sitting in a cyber cafe in Garhmukteshwar,' she said in her statement.

She didn't remember the contents of the affidavit, she said, but she changed her name to Bushra. 'I went to a cyber cafe in Garhmukteshwar alone,' she recollected. She took a bus from Hapur to get there on 31 July 2014. Shallu filed the affidavit in Garhmukteshwar so that her relatives in and around Hapur would not learn that she had converted to Islam. After submitting the affidavit, she returned to Hapur and stayed with a school friend (unnamed in the statement) overnight. The next day, she went to meet Kalim at the college, but couldn't find him there.

Today, Shallu lives happily with her husband and is the mother of a little girl. She hopes the past will not cast a shadow on her future.

MEERUT

CHETNA DEVI AND THE HINDU ARMY

The year 2030, according to the predictions of Chetna Devi, is when Muslims in this country will outnumber Hindus since 'they reproduce like pests.' This will happen sooner than we think, she says. Hindus will be hunted down and made refugees in their own motherland by 'majoritarian' Muslims, she believes, because in a land where Muslims dominate, no other religion is allowed to exist. She claims to understand their game plan; their hidden agenda to usurp Bharatvarsha from Hindus. And to prepare for this distinct eventuality, she wants Hindus— usually a peaceful community, she said—to take up arms and prepare for a war of faith that will preserve their religion and their existence. To this end, she trains women and children in weaponry, including bows and arrows, swords and even guns. Such training centres are called akhadas.

Chetna Devi is known to the world as Yati Maa Chetnanand Saraswati, head of a Meerut-based outfit called Akhand Hindustan Morcha. She is one of the most

charismatic and prominent religious leaders in a region
that has produced many like her.

Meeting her was a bit of a challenge, though. Not
because she didn't want to meet us and discuss her
worldview, but because the directions she gave us to her
house were utterly convoluted. That, we were to realise
later, was the only ambiguity we would experience in
dealing with her. It took us an hour longer than we had
anticipated to get to her home, which we finally managed
with the help of her neighbours. Chetna Devi is popular in
her neighbourhood. She is both a lawyer and a religious
leader, which is a rare but useful combination of talents,
and one that makes it difficult to ignore her.

We eventually found her independent double-storied
house sandwiched between two other houses in a corner
plot, surrounded by a high wall. Iron gates opened into a
small courtyard ornamented with a few potted plants, and
clothes were drying on washing lines. To all appearances, it
was a quintessentially middle class home in this district of
a million-plus people.

We were welcomed in. Chetna Devi was seated on a
long sofa in the living room. She seemed amiable, even
charming. This was a surprise: we had watched videos
on social media sites in which she, with the eloquence
of a demagogue, denounced Muslims as sub-humans and
the greatest threat to Hinduism (read civilisation). Chetna
Devi advocates violence as a survival tactic, arms women
and children to 'meet all eventualities', and vociferously
implores Hindus to join her organisation if they want to
live a decent life.

At home, she was in what seemed to be a nightie—a
loose orange robe, one of her legs in a plaster cast from

knee to heel. She had broken her leg, but her spirit, as was evident, was undiminished. We were to realise that her pain threshold is very high: she could function properly in a condition that would force many others to rest. She has some serious health issues too, she informed us as she swallowed pills. She has acute asthmatic bronchitis and frequently needs to steady her breathing with a nebuliser. But this does not stop her from espousing her views loud and clear.

We had first heard about Chetna Devi in connection with Shallu, the poster figure for love jihad. Chetna had helped the family 'rescue' Shallu from marrying Kalim. She has provided similar services to many Hindus families, all cases of love jihad. In her quest to save Hinduism, in fact, Chetna is particularly concerned with love jihad.

According to the propaganda, love jihad is the act of a Muslim man enticing a Hindu girl into a relationship and then marrying her. In the process, the girl is converted to Islam. And since a Muslim man is legally allowed four wives, he can repeat the process several times. Many fertile Hindu girls are thus converted to Islam and bear Muslim children. This means Hindus are deprived of potential mothers. If this larger strategy succeeds, there won't be enough Hindu women left to give birth to Hindu children.

For Chetna, love jihad is a sinister socio-religious plot by one religion against another. Though her own personality is pretty tough, Chetna feels young Hindu girls are gullible and vulnerable, easy prey for 'sensuous' Muslim men.

That Muslim men are sensuous is also the fault of their faith, she says. In what she claims is a scientific theory, she says that, since Muslims as a community are relatively poor, they live in small houses without privacy. Young children, therefore, witness their parents in the act of sex very early on. Since they are initiated into sexual intimacy early, they are better at satisfying a woman's desire. Therefore, if a Hindu girl experiences intimacy with a Muslim boy, she falls madly in love, and even the honour of her family becomes a secondary consideration.

I smiled and said, 'It's not fair to call only Muslim men sensuous.'

She didn't get the joke and said, 'There is a reason for it. Sex is not taboo in a Muslim family. And the family encourages them to trap Hindu girls.'

I didn't try to convince her that her castigation of Muslim men as irresistible is actually a compliment to them, and that her characterisation of Hindu girls as innocent and gullible is actually criticism. The implication, of course, is that Hindu girls don't have minds of their own, and therefore, are prone to being manipulated. However, when it comes to Shallu, these conclusions are not borne out by the facts. Shallu was fiercely independent and sure of her mind in the face of enormous social and family pressure, even death threats.

Chetna blamed Shallu's family for the young woman's actions. Since she made herself responsible for getting Shallu back, she knows the family well. Tyagi, Shallu's father, 'is an alcoholic', said Chetna. 'He couldn't keep his flock together.' Since the family didn't pursue the matter in court, their outrage in front of the media was mere drama, Chetna concluded in her matter-of-fact manner.

Shallu's younger sister stayed with Chetna for weeks before she returned to her family home, she said, because

Chetna and her husband wanted to ensure that this young woman would not repeat her sister's mistake. 'She was in love with the same man as her older sister,' Chetna repeated, as if to say, can you believe it? Chetna claims that Kalim was having an affair with both sisters, each madly in love with him. Chetna and her husband had to ensure that the younger girl did not elope with Kalim. They counselled her and even used force in their effort to de-indoctrinate her, present reason to her, rescue her life.

Many such girls, Chetna claimed, have sought her help. In her experience, love jihad is a dangerous game. Muslims are innovative in the ways they employ to destroy the Hindu religion, she says, and she lists various types of jihad.

Population jihad: Each married Muslim couple should produce as many children as possible so that one day, not too far in the future, Muslims will outnumber Hindus.

Rape jihad: Thankfully, still not practiced extensively, this means that videos are made of girls being raped. These girls are then blackmailed into submission.

Land jihad: In other words, ghettoisation.

I decided to confront her. 'I'm being the devil's advocate,' I said. 'I have questions to ask. You may not like them. But may I ask?'

'Go ahead. I know your questions,' she retorted.

'You see sinister designs in every action and blame a religion for it. Are you paranoid?'

'The Hindus are sleeping. The way things are these days, it will only culminate in nar-shaghar or mass extermination. Look what happened in Kashmir. Lakhs of Hindus were hounded out of their homes. The situation was bad and is getting worse.'

Chetna Devi sure speaks her mind. As far as she is concerned, there is nothing to hide. But her beliefs are problematic. 'Kill to live,' is her prescription for her fellow Hindus. As a lawyer, she is aware she is going against the ideal of secularism enshrined in the Constitution of India. But she is not apologetic. If anything, she considers herself a reformer. Ushering in a new way of life means displacing the established set-up of the nation. Her convictions are so strong that she can't even see other kinds of beliefs, let alone recognise or accept them.

'I have nothing to hide,' she asserted in Hindi, the language of our conversation. In her late thirties, Chetna is married and the mother of two teenage girls. She is strict with the people around her and has strong leadership qualities. People listen to her. Women twice her age touch her feet in reverence. In her day-to-day life, she is a pleasant person, gracious with a retinue of people who believe she is the chosen one. She leads by example and is a tireless worker.

At home, when you're not talking about her politics, she is affable and hospitable. We were served tea, snacks and halwa as we chatted about this and that.

The moment we started a conversation about her beliefs, Chetna Devi transformed. She has no ambition for electoral politics, she said, but she feels responsible for the preservation of the faith she believes in.

I had promised her right at the start of our meeting that we would present her side of the story and her point of view no matter what our own beliefs may be. She was eager to speak, for our brief to her had been simple: We want to understand what you stand for and why you are doing what you're trying to do. What are your politics? Are they the politics of hate?

Despite her overall mild manner, she stated contemptuously: 'I don't care whether you agree with me or not.' Her demeanour changed when she began speaking, her lips tightened, and she became that person we had watched on YouTube videos, stating with utter conviction that Hinduism is facing an existential crisis created by the burgeoning Muslim population, and that the minority appeasement policy of the government will cost us all dearly.

She has made some intelligent political alliances. We were not surprised to learn that she had supported the Bharatiya Janata Party (BJP) in the general elections of 2014, but her support of them cannot be taken for granted. She wants the political forces to align with her cherished cause. She is not happy with the Modi–Yogi combine; they have done too little to impress her. 'I don't need them. They are politicians and I'm God's person,' she asserted. The BJP, she said, used her organisation for political gain, but does not believe in her extreme political views. 'The BJP promised us help, and we secured them votes. At least two hundred thousand of our supporters voted for them, but they have done nothing on the ground,' she said. On the contrary, she added, the Yogi Adityanath government in BJP-ruled Uttar Pradesh filed an FIR against her guru, Narsinghananda Saraswati, and prevented him from leading a procession.

'We functioned without much trouble during the time of Akhilesh Yadav (the Samajwadi Party chief minister of

Uttar Pradesh before Yogi Adityanath),' she said. This was news to us. Ardent Hindu fundamentalists are not on the same page as the BJP? Really? 'They used us for votes.' Chetna Devi says baldly.

We suggested that her single-minded dedication could be a liability for the BJP, and she concurred. Because Chetna Devi is not seeking power, her agenda is unfinished and her resolve has not diminished in the least. The Ram temple in Ayodhya is still not a reality, she pointed out, and that is an example of how the BJP is not serious about its promises. She was referring to the demolition of the sixteenth-century Babri mosque in Ayodhya—some seven hundred kilometres from her city—on 6 December 1992. The fall of the mosque was alleged to have been politically instigated—that a large group of Hindu activists of the Vishwa Hindu Parishad (VHP) and its allied organisations, after a political rally at the site, turned violent. They demolished the mosque, brick by brick, and even removed the debris from the site.

The containment of Muslims is another issue she feels the BJP is yet to deliver on. Now, after Narendra Modi's first term as prime minister has ended, she is fairly disillusioned.

Chetna displays not an iota of doubt. She's a leader. And she's in control. She has initiative and drive. And she's not driven by political ambition. Chetna sees herself as a messiah, the saviour. Her support base is growing. She has two hundred and fifty thousand followers now.

Radical Hindu organisations like the VHP and Bajrang Dal make tall claims to the media, but don't actually act on the ground, said Chetna Devi. It is organisations like hers that are actually active in organising Hindus against the impending threat of Muslim dominance.

Of course, an impression had been created that the BJP is the defender of the faith, thanks to isolated yet significant incidents such as cow vigilantism and love jihad. But after the elections were over, these issues were allowed to simmer down. Chetna hates it that her concerns are politicised for votes, and is amazed that, despite eight hundred years of Muslim rule, Hindus, as a community, have not learnt their lesson. She doesn't understand why people can't see something that is so clearly visible.

Hindus are easy prey, she said, for apart from being mild people, we lack naitikbal—moral force. This is the crisis of Hinduism. She is here to show the way out of this crisis. Chetna is the Hindus' self-appointed guide. And as the guide or guru, she is a disciplinarian. Her followers train together as a community, focusing not only on the body, but also, the mind. Any sense of individuality is curbed. 'People should think about the community. We want all, especially the women, to come forward and prepare for the worst. Women should learn to wield a sword,' said Chetna.

'I'm not dependent on the government,' Chetna says. She has her own area of influence, her own little army, and there are many like-minded people in the region. But the current problem is the fast-growing Muslim population, and there, she does ask for government help. 'While Hindus should be encouraged to have more children, there should be strict population control among the Muslims,' she said.

And when she is reminded about the law of the land, the Constitution of India that guarantees the right to equality, Chetna gets even more fired up.

'I'm not scared. I welcome death. It's a resting place. We will keep taking birth and keep up the fight. A struggle for my religion is not a crime. I'm not scared of anyone!'

Chetna Devi demands an extra-constitutional struggle that no political party can openly support. Not that the BJP treats the Constitution as sacrosanct. Its backers, the Hindu fundamentalist organisation Rashtriya Swayamsevak Sangh (RSS), have long stood for the idea of Akhand Bharat—an idealised united India based on an ancient past in which borders did not exist, and which would include the modern nations of Pakistan, Bangladesh, Afghanistan, Myanmar, Sri Lanka and Tibet. The in-house publication of the RSS, *Suruchi Prakashan*, published a map of this extended nation titled *Punya Bhoomi Bharat* or *Sacred India*. In this map, Afghanistan is referred to as 'Upganathan', while its capital Kabul is 'Kubha Nagar', Peshawar is 'Purushpur', Multan is 'Moolsthan' and Tibet is referred to as 'Trivishtap'. In the east, Myanmar is called 'Brahmadesh' and in the south, Sri Lanka is 'Singhaldweep'. As for Pakistan and Bangladesh, their integration into India simply returns the country to its pre-Independence undivided state.

For the BJP, renaming is akin to reclaiming. That's why, in BJP-ruled states, several streets, localities and cities have been renamed. For instance, my home town Allahabad, which is derived from two Urdu words Allaha-aabaad, literally meaning 'established by Allah', is now called Prayag Raj. Renaming places and rewriting history seem to go hand in hand. Having said that, I must confess that I would be happy if fewer places were named after the Nehru–Gandhi family. Though India's first prime minister, Jawaharlal Nehru, was a great man, and his daughter Indira Gandhi and grandson Rajiv Gandhi were popular prime ministers, India has no dearth of eminent people who could lend their names to towns and institutions. The freedom struggle against British colonialism, after all, was a popular movement across the subcontinent, and not the work of just a few families.

We visited Chetna several times in the course of our travels. She was curious about us, our motives, and made a thorough enquiry into my life, and looked up my profile on Facebook. Chetna even hinted that she knows more about me than I think she does. I wasn't perturbed, because there was nothing secret about our endeavour.

We always met in her L-shaped drawing room. It has saffron-painted walls, and is packed with oversized sofas covered with bed sheets. Many of these sofas double up as beds—Chetna Devi has many visitors, and quite a number stay the night. There is a fridge next to the kitchen door and a big aquarium at the far end of the room, crowded with fairly big fish. Light streams in through the big windows behind the sofa she sits on. A large picture of Lord Krishna graces one wall.

Chetna was always focused when we spoke. It does not disturb her that her love for her fellow Hindus is fuelled by hatred for Muslims. Indeed, hatred seems to be the guiding force of her myopic worldview. Her hate is genuine, much like true love. She isn't faking it for some political convenience. And I can't help but empathise with her: she is so wrong, but her convictions are the gospel truth to her, and she is tormented by them every moment of her life. All this hatred has become her life force.

She explains her fear of living in a Muslim-majority India in various ways. There will be a Muslim prime minister, and that will almost instantly make Hindus refugees in their own country. She draws out this doomsday scenario with all the drama of a theatre performer. You might wonder, given the strength of her feeling for the victimised Hindus of the future, whether she could spare some of that empathy for the Muslims of the present. Attacked for the most frivolous of reasons, now that the BJP is in power, Muslims in India today certainly feel they are refugees in their own country. But, no. That was asking Chetna Devi for too much.

We politely tested her hypothesis in the light of history. Gently, we reminded her of certain facts: that India had been ruled by the British and before them, by Muslim rulers for a good millennium. Neither the British nor the Muslims had been the majority community; on the contrary, they had been minuscule minorities. Yet, they managed to rule. And while their various reigns had mixed results, Hinduism not only persisted, but assimilated various other influences over the centuries while retaining its essential character.

'Islam is a problem,' she persisted, baffled that we could not see this simple fact that she was trying to hammer into our minds. 'See what's happening all over the world. Muslims are always part of conflict. Terrorism and Islam are synonymous. This is an existential battle for Hindus. By 2030, Muslims will be the majority community in India, and Hindus will be slaughtered on the streets,' she reiterated.

History shows that this is unlikely to happen, we pointed out. 'But what if it happens? We can't say, sorry, we're not prepared, and ready ourselves to die. We should be able to defend ourselves against any eventuality. And to do that, we have to start preparing now.' Her demagoguery is not born out of love for Hinduism but hate for Islam.

When the tea and snacks arrived, Chetna's demeanour changed again. She became the most generous host; we shared jokes while sipping tea. The snacks were wholesome, almost a meal, and we were always hungry.

Her husband looks much older than her: fairly frail, with a moustache on his bony face. He has a deep, husky voice, and over the years, has become a keen believer in his wife's convictions. He interrupted her often, adding unnecessary details to what she said. Chetna ignored him sometimes, and continued with her sermons as he simultaneously tried to substantiate his wife's arguments.

She has many arguments, many stories to tell. A good orator, she speaks in her drawing room the way she would speak from the podium to a gathering of supporters. Chetna has narrated this story hundreds of times, and each time, she reinforces the ideas for herself as much as she does for others, so there is no escape. She is a captive to her own worldview.

Chetna claims to know history. The people of the monotheistic religion, she says, have a fairly aggressive history of propagating their faith. In India, they are waiting for the right moment to strike. A sort of clash of civilisations will ensue, and the weak Hindus should be ready to face the challenge by arming themselves in preparation. Her vision of the future is dark and her fears are real—if you don't agree with her, that's your problem. She's not seeking support or approval. It's a question of life and death.

The first formidable challenge to Chetna's worldview came from her own father. He was also a lawyer in Meerut and many of his clients were Muslims. Chetna started her legal practice as an apprentice to her father. She was rude and harsh to her father's Muslim clients and many of them were justifiably antagonised. Her father tried to counsel his rebellious daughter, with little success. Finally, he asked her to leave. She stayed away from her father for many years, with no contact between them, despite living in the same town. But towards the end of his life, she claims, her father did understand what she was fighting for.

Her leg was in a plaster and she was in pain, but Chetna drove us to her ashram to meet her guru Narsinghananda Saraswati. The ashram is an hour's drive from her home. Its closest town is Hapur. A serpentine, metalled road led us to Dasna Devi Mandir, the ashram. A banner tied across the entrance states in Hindi: 'This is a sacred place for Hindus. Muslims are not allowed.'

Outside the gate, as Raul was photographing the absurd and hateful banner, we met a Muslim man wearing a skull cap. He identified himself as a local trader. 'We lived here happily for centuries,' he said with anger and contempt. 'This is what they have to tell us. They came (referring to the ashram) here and now, want to make us fight. Love and brotherhood are things of the past.' He was dejected. 'What's the point of taking pictures?' he asked. 'You're promoting them. They're an insult to me and you, to every Indian.'

I worry that, though he has every reason to feel offended and hurt, this sense of dejection and resignation to the new reality of India will only embolden people like Chetna. But what can he do? The community's survival tactics, as counselled by its elders, is to lie low and swallow insults.

Muslims tell the young ones, their sons and daughters, to negotiate this tricky phase as frogs do when they hibernate

Shallu at her home in Sarawaha. At the time of the photograph, the 'love jihad' story was all over the news, she was being held captive by her own family, had converted to Islam and adopted the name 'Bushra' to marry Kalim.

In Sarawaha, a student walks by the madrassa where Shallu used to teach English. Nearby, a mosque and a temple coexist peacefully.

Chetna Devi, known to the world as Yati Maa Chetnanand Saraswati, is the head of a Meerut-based outfit called Akhand Hindustan Morcha.

The image was taken at the ashram run by Chetna Devi in Hapur.

in the winter. No parent wants their son or daughter to be caught in the crossfire and die an early death. To survive is the most basic need. When you know your adversary has political patronage, you try to avoid conflict. Some hot-blooded young men don't subscribe to this passivity, but they are few and far between.

Chetna is satisfied that Hindus—the underdogs—have been able to instil fear among Muslims. To her, though, this silence is ominous: 'They are busy multiplying,' she said. Escorted into the ashram by Chetna, we were treated with respect. A dusty road ended in a gateway, which opened onto a big courtyard. There was a small temple on the right, and in front of it, was the sculpture of a crouching lion. A lion was buried inside this sculpture, we were told. A lion who had defended the faith.

Not far from the sculpture, people sang devotional songs. In the covered area of the courtyard, opposite the temple, there was a big fire pit for yagnas. Yagnas are a regular feature here, we were told, and sometimes, they last for twenty-four hours. The ashram also conducts shastra-puja, in which arms and ammunition are worshipped. It has katha, or storytelling sessions to explain the scriptures and complex issues in a simple language, so that people from all walks of life can understand them. The ashram claimed that it had doctors and engineers among its ardent supporters and that caste was no barrier: all Hindus are encouraged to participate, whether they are Gujjar or Yadav or Mochi or Baniya.

Chetna made some enquiries, and we crossed the courtyard to the far end, where another big enclosure was being constructed: a hall for devotees to assemble and pray. In the middle, sitting with others in a circle of plastic chairs, was Chetna's guru.

The other men looked like local politicians. They were introduced to me as people faithful to the cause espoused by Chetna Devi. She left us to attend to her work, while I had a conversation with Guruji over a cup of tea.

In his mid-fifties, with a stocky body and a trimmed beard on a round face, Guruji spoke in monosyllables, often distracted by the others around us. Chetna had already informed me that an FIR had been registered against Guruji and some of his supporters, and that he might have to go to jail. He had led a procession on Hanuman Jayanti even though local authorities had denied them permission. I thought this was an appropriate issue with which to start the conversation.

'We never needed permission in the past,' Guruji said, and since he has been organising these processions for twelve years now, his outfit predates the Modi and Yogi governments. He holds the BJP government responsible for the FIR against him.

'This government seems to be pro-Muslim,' Guruji said. While he is not allowed to lead a procession, Muslims are allowed to hold public events where they chant anti-India slogans like 'Pakistan Zindabad' in the heart of Delhi.

Now, that's just not true. In Delhi's Jawaharlal Nehru University, in western UP's Hapur and in Aligarh Muslim University (AMU), cases were registered against those who allegedly raised anti-India slogans. As many as nine students of AMU were served notice by the university administration, and an FIR was registered by name against two students for raising slogans of azadi (freedom) after a 'terrorist' (Kashmiri youth) was killed in an encounter with security forces in October 2018.

But Guruji believes that, instead of putting these 'anti-nationals' (read Muslims) behind bars, they were provided with security. He accused the Yogi government of patronising minorities, particularly Muslims.

Though Guruji had been denied permission to take out the annual procession, he led it anyway. The superintendent of police ordered a lathi charge to disperse his followers. 'I was detained for instigating communal violence. And I'm ready to go, again and again,' Guruji declared.

Guruji has led an interesting life. His father was a communist who ensured that his son got a good education. In the 1980s, Guruji went to Russia to study engineering. After his course ended, he took time off and travelled extensively in Europe. He stayed for nine years in Russia and other European countries and returned to India in the mid-1990s.

He was disenchanted with life in general, and sought answers to his existential dilemmas. He claimed to have studied various religions, including Islam. The late 1990s were years of introspection. He studied the Quran and even claimed to have spent some time in a madrassa to learn about the religion he now hates.

'I have no confusion about it. Islam is a problem all over the world. It would not be wrong to call it a dangerous ailment. The world should be made aware of it. That's what I'm doing,' he said.

In our conversation, he repeated thoughts that Chetna had already spoken of in detail. His perspective, though, was global. 'They are growing in number all over the world. There should be strong legislation to prevent their proliferation,' he said, as though Muslims were nuclear arms. 'Increasing their population is a good strategy for them,' he said. And we should be open to learning good things even from our enemies. 'Hindus, too, should have many children,' he prescribed. India has a population of a billion plus and growing. But a population explosion is not a concern for Guruji as long as Hindus account for it.

'Syria, Iraq, Bangladesh and Pakistan, all under the grip of Wahabism, a fundamentalist form of Islam, are the countries where trouble resides,' he said. 'They have become terror factories. They export terror all over the world and destroy themselves in the process. Unless Islamist jihad is uprooted from the world, peaceful growth is not possible. This will be the fate of India if we don't stop Muslims from proliferating,' he said. 'When Muslims are the majority, prosperity is not possible. It's a question of survival for Hindus,' he explained.

This calls for direct action, he said, but the manobal or self-confidence of the government is low. An ardent critic of the RSS, Guruji explained that without having done anything, the RSS wants to show the world how much they have done for Hindus. 'After grabbing power, they have become like the Congress,' he said. He accused the Congress Party of pampering Muslims, of feeding a monster.

To make his point, he made an interesting comparison. 'Before coming to power, the RSS claimed to be supporters of Savarkar (Vinayak Damodar Savarkar, known as Veer Savarkar, a freedom fighter and the man who formulated the philosophy of Hindutva). And after grabbing power, they provide their support to (Mahatma) Gandhi.' The RSS had been accused of being part of a conspiracy to assassinate Mohandas Karamchand Gandhi. 'Modi, it seems, works for Muslims,' Guruji quipped. A mahant for the last twelve years, Guruji lives in the ashram. He is fearless even as he anticipates an imminent arrest. 'I take full responsibility for my actions,' he said.

'After I go to jail, Chetna will be the leader,' he added, speaking a little louder so that all those present could hear him clearly. And then, he said, with a tinge of nostalgia, 'I have played my innings. I have tried my best (to cause a rift between the two communities), but have failed. It's for Chetna to lead now and do what is necessary.'

Guruji is married. Like Narendra Modi, he left his wife and the comfort of his family for a larger cause. He has two sons, though, who lead a life very different from his. He was forthright: 'My family doesn't agree with me and I don't have their support.' He lives like an ascetic in a single room.

Chetna joined us at last, a smile lighting up her face as she listened to her guruji. Then, she explained the organisation's various programmes to train Hindus to use arms. 'I regret that you were not there when the firing was taught,' she said. 'Now, we have stopped it because of the authorities. But we will invite you when it's held next.'

As shadows covered the courtyard late in the day, an old woman rushed to Chetna and touched her feet. They had a long chat. 'I can't get over my anger,' the woman said. To which Chetna retorted, 'I have sacrificed everything at the feet of Mother Durga, except the anger. This anger will propel a change.'

And then, she looked at me, standing a few feet away, and started a sermon on why anger is good. 'Mother Durga couldn't have killed so many demons had she not been angry. Anger means things affect you. And when you're unhappy about things, you work towards changing them,' she said.

'Is unhappiness the same as anger?' I interrupted.

She didn't answer the question. Instead, she issued a statement. 'I may look happy, but there's a reservoir of anger inside me. This anger is reserved for the enemy.'

MEERUT

THE AFTERMATH OF
LOVE JIHAD

Sanauallah Khan's family does not trust us. As far as they are concerned, Raul and I—two strangers claiming to be journalists—are akin to agents from the Central Bureau of Investigation, here to put Sanauallah through a trial by media all over again.

Sanauallah is perhaps the most important person in this book. Things went horribly wrong for him for no fathomable reason, aside from the fact that he is a thinking man who speaks his mind and is far more liberal than many of his family members.

Despite being wronged by the system, he trusts people. He is not bitter, and he doesn't take what happened to him personally. Perhaps, he understands the larger picture: that what happened was not about him, but about politics. And he was caught in this politics because he was in the wrong place at the wrong time. That explains why he was always forthright with us, though his family begged him to stay quiet.

Raul wanted a family picture with Sanauallah, his wife Samar Jahan, and their four sons and two daughters.

Sanauallah's younger brother and his family and their octogenarian father stay with him. No one wanted a family picture to be taken by two strangers who claimed to be journalists. Sanauallah only managed to persuade his wife and their youngest son, aged ten, to pose for us.

His house has two doors, one broad and ornate with carvings and brass studs, like that of a haveli in Rajasthan; the other fairly diminutive. The two doors are next to each other, separated only by a pillar, and open into the same courtyard. A wall once divided the courtyard, which explains the two doors. But now that has been demolished. Adversity has cemented the family bond in the same way that the government's treatment of Muslims as second-class citizens has acted as an adhesive within the community.

The house has been built incrementally over the last century, each generation adding to what existed. Certain parts of the house, such as the facade, could even be a few hundred years old. There once were mud huts within the walls, but in the last few decades, these have been replaced by concrete structures. The courtyard has two separate sets of rooms, each occupied by one brother. Sanauallah's family live in a big room that leads to a smaller one which is used as a store for grain, which is stocked in big, cylindrical metal containers. The larger room, with its cement floor and cement walls, is where his immediate family lives. There are several sleeping cots scattered about, and at the far right, there is a wooden bed, low and small, shining, as though oil has been spilled on it, with a gas stove placed on top. This is an elevated kitchen inside the room; I thought it could be a huge fire risk.

We were admitted into these private quarters because it was the only place we could take the photograph we wanted. Raul had suggested that the outer room, where the family receives guests, would be a nice place for a picture of the couple. But Sanauallah's father and brother sat at the entrance of the room, which made it impossible for Samar Jahan to come out with her face uncovered. The custom of purdah is strictly followed in this home. And Sanauallah's family did not want the photograph to be taken anyway. Sanauallah tried to persuade them to allow photographs. After an hour, he gave up and led us to his room.

He took all this trouble because he wanted his side of the story to be known to the world. Sanauallah Khan, a fine example of all that is wrong with India's criminal justice system, had a lot to say.

Sanauallah was one of the five main accused in the love-jihad case that captured the imagination of the whole nation—the story of Shallu and Kalim.

The case was widely reported, but some facts were muddled in the media's high-decibel campaign to present a certain picture to the public. Without examining the merits of the case, we found that the media-presented picture was misleading.

The first time we met Sanauallah, he was seated on a wooden cot in the middle of a big, dark room with a bare cement roof, floor and walls. Light filtered in from an open door and two windows, and dust danced in the beams of light. There was something in the darkness inside the room that chilled us to the bone. There was a repressive silence, and the atmosphere was sombre.

Sanauallah was staring at his feet, rubbing the floor and stirring up dust. He looked up and fixed his gaze on the open door. There was resistance there. He wanted to talk, but was also reluctant to speak. Talking was his only respite from pent-up emotions, from the sense of injustice corroding him. But talking also meant reliving the trauma.

On his slandered frame hung a loose, soiled salwar kameez. He looked weak and dejected. Talking about the horrors that he, his wife Samar Jahan and their six children faced, was hard. The pain of being a Muslim in India was strong in him. On this visit and others that we would make in the next few months, he repeated over and over again that India was his motherland, he was not going anywhere, and where would he go? It is unfortunate that he had to make that assertion.

A resident of Sarawaha, Sanauallah is a relatively affluent fruit and potatoes farmer–trader. He is a man interested in life, who enjoys connecting dots and arriving at a logical conclusion. He is educated enough to utter a few sentences in English, and a wise, reasonable man. He keeps up with the news and is articulate about various issues, especially the condition of his village, the employment scenario or the lack of it. 'Why are younger people fleeing the village?' he asked. 'Farming is the worst profession in the country, and the farmer is the most despised of all professionals,' he said.

He is well known in Sarawaha and plays a vital role in local politics. He is not quite a kingmaker, but he's close to being one because he is capable of articulating his thoughts even on complex issues, and can, thus, influence how people think. This ought to make him an asset for any local politician he may support, but he usually corrodes the politicians' support bases rather than adding to them.

His position in the village is probably what opened him up to accusations of 'masterminding' love jihad in the region. This was asserted despite his repeated clarification that he had no connection with Shallu or her family: he wasn't a neighbour, none of his children went to school with Shallu or her siblings and he wasn't a colleague at the madrassa where Shallu was a teacher. He was acquainted with Shallu's father, but that was simply because they lived in the same village. They weren't strangers, nor were they friends.

There are various versions of Sanauallah's role in the crime. Since it was assumed that Shallu could only have taken the major step of eloping with and marrying a Muslim if she had been under the influence of someone else, Sanauallah was the perfect candidate to be that someone else. He was a glib talker. Who else could convince Shallu to marry a Muslim?

Influencing a person, whether consciously or unconsciously, is very different from persuading a person to do something. Mahatma Gandhi influenced a nation—and the whole world. Many followed him, some did not. Some of those were vehemently opposed to him; they even killed him. But his ability to influence others didn't make Gandhi a criminal.

As far as this case is concerned, Sanauallah wasn't even aware that Shallu and Kalim were having a secret affair. He could not have encouraged the two. Shallu's testimony didn't even name him.

But Sanauallah was accused of far more sinister crimes than simply being a bad influence. He was allegedly one of the men who joined Kalim in gang-raping Shallu. The FIR named him and four others: his wife Samar Jahan; one Nawab Ali, Sanauallah's friend who later preached the

Gita in jail; Shallu's friend and confidante Nishad, who had hosted her when she escaped her parents' home fearing for her life; and Kalim, of course.

The FIR was based on the complaint filed by Shallu's family, and had several inconsistencies. As the local press pointed out, the police version kept changing. The FIR about the alleged kidnapping and gang-rape of Shallu on 23 July was registered on 3 August 2014. As you have seen in an earlier chapter, the police station at Kharkhoda was pressured to register a certain FIR. Later, it came to light that the alleged kidnapping did not happen on 23 July. The girl was back home on 27 July. And on 12 August, the national Hindi daily *Amar Ujala* reported that the victim said in her statement to the doctor that she was gang-raped on 29 July and had been kidnapped the same day. But such contradictions are part of the narrative of any concocted story.

～

Sanauallah remained in jail for eight months, Samar Jahan even longer, nearly a year. She was charged with abetting the crime and was refused bail several times for 'technical' reasons.

While the parents were jailed, their four sons and two daughters were looked after by the members of Sanauallah's extended family. But they were no substitute for parents. The youngest child, a boy, was not yet three at the time. All of them were aware of what their parents had been accused of doing, especially their father: raping a local girl. They knew he would never do such a thing. And they were filled with questions.

Why their mother and father? The answer was not difficult to find. They were Muslims. But why only them when other Muslim families also resided in the village? Perhaps because they were too poor to cause a political stir, too inconspicuous and, therefore, safe. Like the other Muslims in the village, Sanauallah's family believed that the new government in power would have no direct bearing on their lives—the lives of poor farmers. They were wrong. Now they know it's tough to be a Muslim in India when a particular Hindu nationalist party comes to power. No one is safe.

Usually, the oldest son, twenty-one-year-old Irfan, attended to us on our visits. We would sit on the veranda just outside the cemented room where we had met Sanauallah for the first time. More often than not, a neighbour of about Sanaullah's age would be eavesdropping, sitting on a cot across the street. The pleasant young man would bring us water in big steel glasses, followed by tea that was too milky and too sweet for my taste.

We never met the second son, Jubair, who is now seventeen years old. The worst affected of all was Jeshan, the third son, who was only thirteen when his parents were taken away. He was too old to forget things and too young to emotionally process the destruction of his family. He was robbed of his childhood. Jeshan is sandwiched between two sisters—Tahzeeb, a year older than him, and Saadiya, a couple of years younger. He would stand by the pillar for hours, staring at nothing in particular. I wasn't even sure if he followed our conversations, though his eyes brimmed with anger. He was an unnerving presence, standing almost as still as a statue, never uttering a word or betraying an emotion. Pain had made him inert.

During the long absence of his parents, this boy was probably mistreated and ridiculed in school. His father featured in all the papers and on television as 'the rapist'. Separated from his mother as well, he would have been angry, fearful, helpless and traumatised by the sheer injustice of it. Unlike his older brother, Jeshan was suspicious, uncomfortable with our presence, unwilling to trust strangers. He betrayed no emotion, but evoked several in others. His glare was unsettling.

Sanauallah admitted that Jeshan was the worst affected of all his children. He's bitter, and that has prevented him from studying and doing anything worthwhile. He likes to be alone, doing nothing in particular. And if Sanauallah says anything, Jeshan snaps back at him.

He now goes to the field to help his family, and is quick to say 'no' to anything that is asked of him. Sanauallah is worried about him. He sent him out of the village, believing that the change would cure him of the trauma. Jeshan went to Delhi, where he worked as an assistant in a food stall somewhere in Zakir Nagar. Like the other jobs he had earlier been pressed into, this did not work out either. He is now back in the village and has settled into his role in the family: the indolent boy with a sharp tongue.

The fourth son, Gazanfar, must be ten years old now, and doesn't remember enough to be traumatised. There is a perpetual smile on his innocent face and he lightens up the sombre mood of the family. He always has a pen tucked into his shirt pocket, and can spell words with ease. As he runs around and plays, he is Sanauallah's smile-generating machine. The father of six is glad that he and his wife are alive and back with their family.

Sanauallah's father often joined us, but he would mostly listen. In his eighties, he is sharp, attentive and concerned. On one occasion, when we discussed the details of the case for over an hour, Sanauallah's father did not utter a word. The family is quiet about what happened. They are glad that Sanauallah is back and will soon start fending for the family. But the older Mr Khan believes Sanauallah should not speak to journalists who more often than not have an agenda, and as a matter of principle, should not be trusted. They learnt this lesson the hard way. Journalists think they know it all and don't bother to investigate closely enough, so what they write is a preconditioned narrative without consideration for the lives and reputations of the people they write about. Sanauallah's family had valid reasons to persuade Sanauallah not to engage with us.

～

The social fabric in this region is tattered with distrust, and religious identity is a hard-to-ignore factor. People tend to be friends only with co-religionists in this little village. Personal association with a Hindu may spell trouble for a Muslim. Sanauallah is an example of that. Even the long friendships of Hindus and Muslims who grew up playing together in the dusty fields are now restrained. '*Musalmaan ke saath na dosti bhali, na bair* (with a Muslim, neither friendship nor enmity is advisable),' a Hindu shopkeeper in the village told me over a cup of tea.

Small bare-brick houses, like matchboxes stashed next to each other, stand on either side of the barely paved road that is just broad enough for a small car to crawl through, twisting and turning every few yards. Older men are seated

on cots in verandas overlooking the road, occupied with
their thoughts and gazing at passersby. People go about
their business in the eerie silence that hangs over these
streets. Men soak up the sun with listless expressions,
women are busy with chores, cow dung punctuates the
streets, and water gushes through an open drain that runs
along the path from Sanauallah's house to the madrassa. It
is only a five-minute walk.

I halted at the barber shop, which was a small room
with two chairs and a mirror stretched full length across
one wall. It also had a washbasin, three boys waiting
for clients, a bench opposite the mirror scattered with
old glossy magazines, and many pictures on the walls. I
decided to get a shave.

A young man named Abdul, twenty years old, talkative
and curious, attended to me. The other two had also
volunteered for the job, but Abdul deputed himself to the
task. He used warm water since I opted for a premium
shave that costs twice as much as the usual ten rupees. On
the wall was the blown-up image of a young man with
a girlish face. Very fair of complexion, he was sporting
an elaborate hairdo—a complex mix of an undercut and
comb-over, with traces of a pompadour. I could see the
reflection of this portrait in the mirror in front of me.

'Can I get a similar cut?' I asked. They laughed. 'You
need longer hair for that,' Abdul finally explained. After a
pause, he took a few breaths so deep that I felt them on
the top of my shoulders. 'Do you recognise the man in
the picture?' he asked. I tried hard but could not. I don't
recognise many of the new Bollywood actors, and the man
in the photo didn't look like any Bollywood or Hollywood
star I knew. I conceded defeat.

'I will give you a hint. The person in the picture is present in this room,' he said with the panache of a street-theatre performer. I looked at him in the mirror and then at the picture. There was some resemblance. 'This is your picture,' I said tentatively. 'Yes, you're right,' he said loudly, as if I had solved a cryptic puzzle. He was a crude version of his picture. The picture manifested Abdul's aspirations, but reality did not match up.

A conversation ensued. The young men of the barber shop were open to the good things of life. Good jeans were the only item on Abdul's bucket list; he was saving up for a pair of Levi's that he planned to buy during the next sale when prices would be slashed to half. His waist size is twenty-eight inches, slightly broader than my thighs.

Now his attention shifted to me. He asked why we were there. I replied vaguely. Everyone had been trying to make sense of what two city people were doing in their village, one of whom held a big camera on his shoulder the way policemen carry Sten guns.

During and after the arrests, there were many policemen stationed here. 'The villagers were so scared,' recollected Sanauallah in one of our many interactions.

'Are you a Muslim?' Abdul asked. This was a crucial question that would determine if this conversation could lead to a friendship. I had to pass the religion test.

'You don't give a Hindu a haircut?' I asked. He wasn't joking. This was a crucial piece of information for him.

'I will cut your hair even if you're a Hindu,' Abdul clarified. 'But why won't you say whether you're a Muslim or a Hindu?'

'Why are you asking this question? Why is it important for you to know my faith? Did I ask you if you're a Hindu?'

He didn't like being confronted by a stranger. He contorted his face to show his displeasure and blurted out, 'I'm a Muslim.' He said this in a way that seemed to assert, 'let there be no confusion about it'.

'I'm a Hindu,' I replied almost instantly in the same tone of voice.

There was silence for some time. Something had changed. Geniality had been replaced by formality. He finished his task, I paid him.

～

Sanauallah had been on the front pages of newspapers all over the country, even more so in the Hindi-speaking belt. He had become a national figure in a few days, representing all that is wrong with Muslims, and why they are a threat to the congenial, malleable, peace-loving, tolerant Hindus who are too mild to fight for their cause. Now, he tries to piece his life together in the benign neglect of the world. Even the villagers have forgotten about it, or at least, the case is not part of the popular discourse. People have settled into their lives, and past events are a warning for the future.

Strangely enough, Sanauallah seemed to miss the limelight. This may seem cruel, but I couldn't escape this feeling every time he interacted with us.

When the media trial of 2014 was in full swing, Sanauallah had been the poster boy of love jihad; the dreaded mastermind. He was in the news daily. Strong media attention, and the public glare that comes from it, is capable of keeping an issue alive in the public domain and can reduce the scope of manipulation by investigative agencies to meet the needs of their political masters. But sometimes, it has the reverse effect: it muzzles the truth by injecting an overdose of popular rhetoric.

To state the obvious, information comes to a journalist with a price tag attached. This is especially true for crime reporters who need a steady flow of information. Cops are their only source, and information is mostly supplied during informal briefings about various ongoing investigations. To secure greater access, some crime reporters make compromises, becoming a tool in the hands of the establishment. They are provided with exclusive information on the cases being investigated, but the information supplied is fairly selective and is often provided to deliberately paint a false picture. The idea is to mislead, sometimes to distract attention from shoddy investigations and incompetence.

Sanauallah was mostly likely a victim of this selective dissemination of information. He was demonised and his reputation was demolished bit-by-bit every day. He is a frail farmer in his fifties, but the media made him out to be a criminal, the mastermind of love jihad, making him the pet figure of hate amongst Hindus.

Posters of Sanauallah were affixed across the city. He was India's most wanted, most dreaded terrorist. There was a reward of five thousand rupees on his head. At a press conference, the Meerut police announced 'Sanauallah—the mastermind—has been arrested.' Allegedly, the police had arrived at a conclusion even before the investigation was completed.

On 6 August 2014, as the case became a media sensation, BJP's state president Laxmikant Bajpai visited

Shallu's family. He was accused by the opposition of communalising the 'honour of mothers and sisters', which indicates that even the opposition believed that Shallu had been kidnapped and gang-raped.

Vajpayee assured Shallu's family that the BJP was with them, and that the victim and her family should seek justice without fear as they would be taken care of by the party. Talking to the media later, Bajpai, who seemed to know more about the case than the police investigating the matter, asserted that the case exposed a conspiracy of organised religious conversion.

V.K. Singh, a former general of the Indian Army, now a minister of state in Prime Minister Narendra Modi's government, also visited Shallu's family and assured them of his support. What message was being sent here? Why were politicians so keenly interested in this particular case when the matter had not even been investigated properly?

A news report in a Hindi newspaper in August 2014 was headlined, 'Gang-rape victim's house was robbed, ransacked', referring to Shallu's house. The first paragraph stated in Hindi: 'In a new turn to the much-discussed gang-rape and religious conversion case, the victim's house was attacked. There was an attempt to burn it down, which caused unrest in the village.'

Further down, the same report clarified: 'However, it was ascertained later that the attack was the outcome of a family feud. The victim's mother accused her brother-in-law (husband's older brother) of many serious offences and said that he wanted to usurp the property and had attacked the house in the absence of her husband.'

This, therefore, had nothing to do with the Shallu and Kalim case. But the story in subsequent paragraphs re-emphasised the position of Shallu's family, which had become the position of the police, that Shallu had been kidnapped and gang-raped.

Towards the end of the same story, the factual position of the case was stated—the fact that should have killed the story itself in the first place—that the 'victim' had falsified all the rhetoric that she had been kidnapped and gang-raped. The story said: 'One month ago, the victim suddenly disappeared from her house and went to the mahila thana (women's police station). She declared that the accused are innocent and that she ran away from her house because of a risk to her life from her own family members.'

So, the facts are there but only at the end, and a reader who only saw the headline, and perhaps, read the first few sentences of the story would have got the wrong message. The media bias in covering love jihad was stark naked.

This bias propagated that Muslim men treat Hindu girls as objects of desire. In this pursuit, the accused Muslim men were together, like the Pakistani cricket team. And the venue of this heinous alleged crime was a madrassa: a place of learning, where religion, theology and Islamic texts are taught to young believers, only to emphasise that they have religious sanction to commit crimes on Hindus, that it is fine to disrespect a woman and disrobe her of her honour if she happens to be Hindu.

But there were holes in the narrative. On the one hand, a series of stories claimed that Shallu was forcibly converted to Islam, and later integrated into Kalim's family. On the other hand, stories said that one of the rapists, Kalim, married her. Such narratives, seething with hatred, were created to spread distrust and provoke communal clashes. And, of course, to polarise votes.

Therefore, Sanauallah wants to talk, for he has a lot to say. Now, however, there are no listeners, no takers for his version of the story. Such as how, though the police claimed he had been arrested after a manhunt, he had no clue that the police was looking for him—he was in a hospital. He explained how the facts of the matter are different from what had been portrayed. We'd hear him out patiently. It made him feel better. He'd call us often during the making of this book, enquiring about our progress.

In a way, Sanauallah is detached from his own miseries. He doesn't like this lull after the storm. Having been covered by the mainstream media for all the wrong reasons, he is now languishing in this dusty village, trying to piece together his life. 'They have left the "mastermind" to die his own death,' he said. To his credit, he is not bitter. Nor is he sceptical. He is just running out of patience.

~

Sanauallah was in jail for eight months, where he met Kalim and got to know him. He had been accused of orchestrating this man's marriage to a Hindu girl. They discussed their intertwined destinies.

It wasn't as though Kalim had not known Shallu, or that the two of them hadn't had an affair. They had wanted to be partners in life, and what was wrong with that? They were committed to each other, and ready to face all the repercussions that came with this decision. Only, they didn't understand the magnitude of the repercussions. They should have known that religion, caste and creed are formidable barriers in their corner of the world, as it is in most of India.

Sanauallah makes this point several times: Kalim and Shallu had something to do with each other, and therefore this case came into being. They did have an inter-faith marriage. So: 'What did I do to be in jail?' In jail, Kalim and Sanauallah would often talk. Kalim was reluctant at first, but progressively opened up. The first few weeks were spent trying to come to terms with what they had been accused of: raping Shallu. This was a rude shock to Kalim who loved her and wanted her to be his wife. Sanauallah was clueless. Good as he was at connecting the dots, it took him a while to understand what was happening. The two came to believe that they were being persecuted for their faith. They felt cornered, but they also gained strength from the knowledge that they were political prisoners.

After the initial shock, the instinct of self-preservation kicked in, and they began to think and devise survival tactics. Sanauallah started to see the bigger picture: that what was happening was not about him, but about creating a certain paranoia within the society and mistrust between two communities that have coexisted for centuries. People were being made to believe that a low-intensity war had been going on, and Sanauallah was being depicted as one of the foot soldiers against Hinduism, corroding it from the inside by inciting Hindu girls to convert and marry Muslim men. He was the victim of a manufactured reality.

This sense of injustice colours Sanauallah's descriptions of his interactions with Kalim. For the first month or so in jail, Kalim was in complete denial. He claimed that he had nothing to do with Shallu. All he would admit was that Shallu was an acquaintance he had met a few times, and that he was being framed.

Kalim is not the first, and nor will he be the last, to disown the love of his life for fear of his life. He was in the eye of a national storm. They read papers, listened to the news on the radio ... they knew they were the faces of the unrest—the love jihadis!

Kalim had come to personify the 'seductive Muslim men' theory propounded by Yati Maa Chetnanand Saraswati, that Muslim men 'cast their charm on hapless Hindu girls who find them difficult to resist'.

After a few weeks of denial, Sanauallah recollected, Kalim started opening up. 'Is loving a person such a big crime?' he wondered.

Kalim finally acknowledged that he knew Shallu very well, though he denied any romantic liaison between them and claimed that it was just friendship—a friendship so close that he started treating Shallu like 'a sister'.

It took Kalim a few more months to finally tell Sanauallah that Shallu wasn't a sister after all. They would occasionally hire a hotel room clandestinely and spend time together, using Kalim's identity card to check into the hotel. However, Kalim still did not acknowledge that he and Shallu had planned to marry.

'Kalim wasn't sure if he'd marry Shallu, he'd say it was just a fling,' Sanauallah recollected.

It was as though imprisonment had given him the space to think and infused in him, the ability to question everything he had believed in so far. While doing time, Sanauallah relived the injustice every moment, and then, felt a sadness that turned into stillness. Perhaps, he tried to contextualise life and find reasons for the present state of affairs. Could the sins of a past life make the present hell?

Often, when logic fails, faith comes into play. Many inmates of that jail were dealing with existential crises of their own making. With the help of jail authorities, they formed an informal group by the name of Om Shanti Programme.

Nawab Ali, who had been jailed because he was a friend of Sanauallah-the-mastermind, was a regular speaker at the Om Shanti Programme. According to Sanauallah, his pet topic of deliberation was the Gita—the sermons Krishna gave to Arjun when the latter got cold feet on the battlefield in the Mahabharata. Ali made his wonderment public: when the creator is one, how come there are so many religions, he asked. He would have realised that, though the destination may be the same, there can be different paths leading to it. And of course, the stakeholders of each of these various paths, cajole and woo travellers to use theirs, telling people that their path is the best or the quickest or the shortest path to God.

The Om Shanti Programme discussed the hidden similarities between Hinduism and Islam. If you turn 'Om' by ninety degrees in the anti-clockwise direction, it reads Allah. Hindu scriptures talk about Kalki, the tenth avatar of Vishnu, who will arrive from the centre of the earth at the end of the Kali Yuga. To some of the Muslims involved in the discussion, Kalki had already arrived from the centre of the earth as predicted, in the form of the prophet Muhammad. Mecca, where he was born, is in the centre of the planet, they argued. Though there is no verifiable proof for this theory, it is a heartening piece of information. Men accused of infringing on the faith of others were talking about rapprochement.

One afternoon, sitting out in the sun, Kalim told Sanauallah that he had accompanied Shallu to the hospital for an abortion, posing as her husband. There is documentary proof with the police. 'There's no iota of doubt that they were in a relationship. They met regularly and the phone records prove it beyond doubt. And then, Kalim helped Shallu get the abortion.' Sanauallah listed on his fingers the things that irrefutably connected Kalim with Shallu right from the start.

'What Shallu's phone records establish is that she was in touch with Kalim, not me. A fact that neither of them deny,' said Sanauallah, agitated. He paused, taking deep breaths, and then added more assertively, 'What's there that connects me to them and this whole episode? There was nothing. There will be nothing. Nothing! Nothing! Nothing!'

Whether Shallu and Kalim's affair was love jihad or not is a good topic for television prime-time debates. What's certain is that the two had an affair, and that Sanauallah had little to do with this affair. Nor did he participate in the gang-rape that never happened. Shallu has time and again clarified that no one raped her and that her relationship with Kalim was consensual.

A year in jail was not only catastrophic for Sanauallah's family but also his livelihood. Many acres of his fruit orchard, something that takes years to establish, were destroyed. He's out of business and it will be many moons before he breaks even. The cost of lawyers has been impossible to bear. He has the support of his extended family, but that's not enough. His life is destroyed and so is his reputation. He was the headline, the face of juicy stories for weeks. Now, he pays the price for having been made a public spectacle of.

The case still exists, is still being tried, even though the matter has been settled for all practical purposes. Sanauallah and the other accused have to present themselves at the district court in Meerut twice a month. It takes more than an hour and a half to get to the court. The lawyers have to be paid as well. The case is proceeding at a snail's pace.

Raul and I joined them one day when they were supposed to attend the court. The matter was not taken up. This was made known to the accused only after they arrived, and they were told to come again in a few days.

'What have I done to be in jail for a year, and have my life destroyed? How will I pay the lawyers when there's not even enough to eat?' asked Sanauallah.

No one is interested in this question. No one is interested in justice. And no one cares that justice has not been done—not the local politicians, not the media, not the police. The case is languishing in a dusty corner of the district court of Meerut.

Sanauallah has no illusions. He's alone in this and will have to go through the grind of a prolonged trial to prove the obvious—if he's ever able to do that.

The only silver lining is that Shallu and Kalim are happily married. Had the Allahabad High Court not come to Shallu's rescue, there is no saying what could have happened to them.

But Sanauallah has no options. He has not been proved innocent in a court of law. The only way out of this crisis is through it.

DEOBAND

THE SCHOOL OF FAITH

In January, we spent a nice, sunny day at Darul Uloom, Deoband. Our contact there was a young local journalist, a practising Muslim known to Raul. He is well connected with the establishment and turned out to be an excellent facilitator, opening many doors for us. Let's call him Aslam.

Aslam is an insider for good reason. He has been tried and tested by the local establishment. Like many young Muslims in the region, he feels victimised because of his faith. His own life experiences and the things he has witnessed have made him bitter. He's fervent when he says that Muslims are not treated well in India and face an existential crisis, especially since 2014 when the BJP came to power. Over a cup of tea, he tells us that Muslims are being victimised in their own country because, as a religious minority, they are a soft target: poorer, less educated and, therefore, vulnerable economically and socially. 'To feel alienated does not feel good,' he said, then took a deep breath and reiterated: 'This is our country as well,' emphasising the words 'as well'.

Aslam's sentiments echoed everywhere in this small, congested town of Deoband. The open drains running alongside the roads, the worn-out buildings, the filth and garbage dumps punctuating the surroundings all reminded me of the town of Vrindavan. The views of the Muslims here is a political discourse. They feel wronged by those in power—those sworn to protect the people of this country irrespective of their community. The government is so powerful that it can coddle one community at the cost of antagonising another, all the while pitching the two against each other. Muslims are projected as a manifestation of evil, and it saddens them as much as it angers them. When I asked questions about the state of the country, I was confronted with their anguish, whether I was talking to a paanwala, a shopkeeper, or the waiter at a restaurant who served us piping hot tea overdosed with sugar and milk.

Aslam's emotions found a release when he spoke to us about this sense of insecurity. It was as if we had touched a raw nerve. It was a sombre beginning to a day in a sombre place where we did a lot of listening. A very affable man, Aslam is also kind. He treated us to homemade food, sweet chai and tasty paan.

Thanks to Aslam, we were allowed inside the Darul Uloom, the hallowed Muslim seminary, at around noon. The arched red-brick gateway leads to an enclosed courtyard. Along the walls on either side are noticeboards cluttered with handouts, pamphlets and posters, all pinned one on top of the other. Many of these notices were in Bengali and Assamese. No one can dispute that Bengalis are the most prolific when it comes to filling bare pages with content, I thought.

Darul Uloom is an important centre of Islamic theology, not only for India but also beyond the frontiers of the subcontinent. It's one of the biggest madrassas in the world, certainly the biggest in Asia, I was told. Initially established as a school, it is now one of the most influential institutions of Islamic discourse in the subcontinent, housing thirty-two departments and administrative offices. Since photography is strictly not allowed inside the campus, this was one of the rare occasions when Raul didn't have his camera bag dangling from his shoulder. He looked odd to me; incomplete. The camera was in the boot of the car.

As we were shown around the campus, we passed an auditorium packed with pupils in their late teens and early twenties. There must have been around a thousand students, all sitting and reading texts in eerie silence. A sort of inaudible buzz filled the room, felt but not heard. Focused on their books, perhaps reading the same texts at the same time, they were isolated from each other in the group, yet connected via what they were reading.

It was a wonderful sight. At that moment, I wanted to shoot a picture; my hand involuntarily grabbed the phone in my jeans pocket. But good sense prevailed, and I didn't do it. Pictures taken by outsiders are not trusted by insiders. Such pictures, they are convinced, will be used by the popular media to present a false image of the institution. Therefore, to be on the safe side, there is a blanket ban on photography except under special conditions.

Unlike many of the smaller madrassas we had been to in the past few months, where much younger children were initiated into Islamic study and the Quran by chanting verses aloud and rocking back and forth to the rhythm, here, the group was fairly still. The whole campus felt like it was hard at work in that silence. This silence was like the numbness caused by fervent emotions; it was a silence created by non-engagement with the material world. The pupils here feel they are destined for the service of the divine and, therefore, they are special. Hundreds of pupils sat in neat files on the floor; every inch of the hall was packed. The maulvis—teachers—were seated on low wooden pedestals, aware of what was going on around them, yet engrossed in their study. One of them looked at us, the intruders, observed us for a few seconds to satisfy his curiosity, and almost immediately resumed reading. Our presence was felt. Intruders dressed in jeans and jackets are not always welcome in this sanctuary. They are a bad omen. At least, that is what I felt in the intent gaze of the people we passed in the corridors lined with worn-out iron almirahs. The almirahs, some fairly disfigured but still standing, are custodians of the past; in their bellies are stored the papers and belongings of the people who serve the institution.

We walked the campus at leisure. The mess that feeds thousands of pupils every day was efficiently organised. Mutton was being cooked in vessels as large as overhead water tanks. The smell of spices and herbs hung in the air, fuelling my appetite. This was like an egalitarian commune where people dressed similarly, followed the same routine, read the same texts, spoke the same language, ate the same food, and lived in equitable spaces. Some were privileged— their beds were next to a window. Each person's individuality seemed to have merged with the overarching identity of the place.

The library on the first floor is huge. One rectangular hall opens into another. The walls of each hall has bookshelves from floor to ceiling, with glass doors like french windows. There are books and scriptures rolled into bundles, all neatly stacked and meticulously catalogued. Of late, the library has started using cataloguing software to manage its books and scriptures. Scriptures and rare texts are being digitised.

There is an exquisite collection of Arabic and Persian scriptures, some more than a thousand years old. In the centre of one hall, display tables with slanting glass tops exhibit rare scriptures, manuscripts, letters and documents. Since Arabic is all Greek to me, I could only marvel at the calligraphy, an advanced art form in itself. Islamic scholars from all over the world come to study here, I was told, to benefit from this reservoir of knowledge.

Apart from the display tables and the bookshelves, the halls are devoid of furniture. There is only a carpet for pupils to sit on while referring to the books. The senior functionaries of the library sit behind a low table with a slanting top, their legs folded beneath them on cotton mattresses and backs supported by thick cylindrical pillows called gau-takiya. They keep a vigilant eye on the halls even as they make entries in thick registers.

They were curious about the unannounced visit of two strangers. One of the librarians, a big fellow with a long white beard and a pleasant, smiling face, engaged us in an elaborate conversation. 'We contribute to nation-building like few institutions could or would,' he said in Hindustani, a complex mix of Urdu and Hindi. 'We provide free education to thousands of pupils, age no bar. This is an institution of great discipline that inculcates moral and ethical values in its pupils and creates responsible, peace-loving, law-abiding citizens.'

Portrait of a girl in Deoband.

Sanauallah at his home in Sarawaha.

The main campus of Darul Uloom, a world-renowned school of Islamic learning in Deoband.

A student engrossed in reading inside the Darul Uloom library.

The librarian cleric was not happy with how the popular media portrays Deoband, but said, 'These opinions are inconsequential to us. We don't threaten anyone. And people are free to believe whatever they want to, as long as they don't force others into believing the same,' he said, and added, 'They say we breed terrorists here. Where are the terrorists? Do you see any?'

Everyone we met wanted to express their anguish. Many of them feel stifled, their voices muffled and views curtailed. It seemed, especially among the older people, that this was not just a reaction to the actions of the government, but a yearning to be allowed to exist as they always had. These days, every aspect of their belief system is being judged and challenged. Orthodox Islam is seen as dangerous to modern life, and therefore, suspected. This is true not just in India but across the world. Islam is seen as the antithesis of a progressive way of life. The religion's attitude towards women is often cited as the reason why the government of the day intervenes in the matters of Muslim faith. Already the triple talaq, also known as talaq-e-biddat, the practice by which a Muslim man can divorce his wife merely by repeating the word 'talaq' three times in quick succession, has been declared a crime. Next on the agenda is a Uniform Civil Code that will no longer allow Indian Muslims the freedom of their personal laws.

I politely told the librarian and others who brought it up that, one, Deoband is certainly not a terror organisation or one that abets terrorism. And two, we were not there to judge them or draw conclusions or issue certificates. The idea was just to be there, get a feel of the place and describe it. Not to conduct an enquiry. And it has to be said that we *had* been given a selective picture of the place before we visited it ourselves. There is nothing wrong with the ban on photography and the restrictions on visitors within the campus. There is a crisis after all: a crisis of trust.

Finally, we were led to the administrative block, where the most senior functionaries work. We met the public relations officer who was sitting behind a desk with a slanting top, his legs folded beneath him on a white mattress. We sat on the floor in front of him. With so many functionaries sitting along the wall in front of their respective desks, it looked like a medieval court-office— high ceilings, light filtering in through the tall open doors and ventilators, dust dancing restlessly in the air, and people walking in and out in a hurry, dealing with urgent matters.

Despite that, the atmosphere was fairly relaxed, which is a sign of people in control, sure of themselves. They understand the situation at hand and will find a solution. They serve their religion with undivided commitment; they help people follow a religion in all its orthodoxy by administering an institution where thousands of pupils are trained to be apostles of the faith. Our questions did not faze them at all.

We were hoping that, while asking questions, I would enter into a conversation with the PRO, develop a rapport and, at an opportune moment, request—or insist on, if need be—permission to take pictures inside the premises.

My first question was: what do the pupils do for a living after they graduate? The reply: Many become priests and serve the religion among the faithful and infidels. Islam has intricate codes of conduct. It is not just about attending to namaz five times a day. A practising Muslim will be concerned about personal hygiene, for instance. It's part of the code of conduct. There's a prescribed way to wash the face and hands, perhaps because the religion originated in a part of the world where water was not plentiful. There's also a prescribed way to copulate and even wash the penis after urination.

Many of my Muslim friends and acquaintances are gregarious and fun loving. But I often feel that in some spheres of life, they keep their distance. They have a larger private sphere that is inaccessible to others. It was quite evident while interacting with the pupils in Deoband that Islam is not just a religion with philosophical underpinnings, it's also a social contract that governs the day-to-day lives of its believers. For the practising Muslim, it can be a detailed personal guide to the performance of daily chores, and Muslims are initiated into this from a very young age so that it becomes an integral part of their existence. Even iconoclasts and rebels find it difficult to break out of the mindset.

Trust in their faith seems to be the overwhelming element at the Darul Uloom, and orthodoxy is the guiding force. While the outside world reacts and attribute motives to the various decrees or fatwas it issues, inside the institution, the decrees are followed without application of mind. Just a few days before we arrived, the Darul Uloom passed a decree that forbids women from wearing designer or slim-fit burqas, as they attract male attention, and are, therefore, against Islam.

A few days after our visit, it forbade Muslim women from marrying into families whose members work in banks, as the income accrued from banking jobs is considered 'haram' or vile, therefore, sinful. Further, in a fatwa last year, Darul Uloom banned Muslims from posting pictures on social media websites. In its most recent edict, Darul Uloom calls the installation of CCTV cameras un-Islamic. Perhaps, this also explains the great resistance to photoshoots inside the campus.

There were some tense moments, but the conversation was largely cordial. The PRO said all the politically correct things and reinforced the obvious, such as, 'Muslims are patriotic people and they love their motherland: Hindustan.' It is a historical fact, he clarified, that the Darul Uloom participated in the freedom struggle against the British Raj. In fact, the institution was established to counter the Christian missionaries who were destroying India's culture. The Darul Uloom movement is a revolution, a movement against the jahani gulami, or intellectual slavery, that was the result of the British Raj in India. And in the one hundred and fifty years of its existence, it has never been subsidised by the government. In that sense, it values its independence.

He was concerned about the government's attitude towards the minority community, but shied away from saying anything that would fuel a controversy.

At some point in the conversation, Raul implored Aslam to add his weight to our request for the permission to shoot. The PRO insisted that it was not possible without clearance from a higher authority, but Raul begged him. He finally conceded, but with a rider. 'I'm allowing you to take photographs on my responsibility. And you have fifteen minutes to take as many pictures as you possibly can,' he said. He was adamant about the time frame, and to make sure we didn't exceed it, he accompanied us for the shoot. But first, Raul had to take a long walk to fetch the camera. Aslam went with him. That left me alone with some of the seniors in the office, and they wanted to participate 'off the record' in a discussion.

We had a fairly open conversation about identity and the demands of an identity, whether religious or otherwise. And the conflict that arises when strong identities compete for the mind's attention. Followers are clients, one must remember. And to hold clients faithful for the rest of their lives, faith has to be ingrained during the formative years so that it lasts a lifetime. To establish one's own faith as superior to all others is part of the process, and this is hardly unique to Islam. This has even led to bloodshed in the past. These are some of the broad contours of our candid conversation.

But one of the clerics emphasised that, in India, people of different faiths have coexisted and prospered together through the ages. India's inclusive culture is our asset, and it was not created after independence, but had been practiced for centuries since ancient and medieval times. There has been discord, but also bonhomie. 'The picture one wants to see is a personal choice,' said a cleric who was soon to retire and seemed exhausted by the rhetoric of conflict.

Another senior functionary, having listened attentively to the discussion, nodding and smiling, looked into my eyes, raised his hands as if in prayer and uttered these words after ensuring that I would protect his identity and only quote him anonymously, 'This has to be said. And we all know it. Even the government of the day knows it. For many years, we have been trying to create discord between Hindus and Muslims. It is, perhaps, a way of asserting our religious identity and the relevance of an institution like Darul. But we have failed and we will continue to fail. Because 90 per cent of Muslims are petty traders and manufacturers, and most of what they produce is consumed by Hindus.'

Anonymity makes people forthright, and we wanted to understand the issue beyond the rhetoric and the posturing. He explained that the economic imperative has bound the two communities together so strongly that even the religious imperative cannot cause sustainable discord. Finding a way to coexist is not an option, it is indispensable. There is no other way. People have to work to feed their families. Faith cannot feed them and faith cannot be sustained on an empty stomach.

I was in tears. It was a moment of epiphany. And now I know for sure, though I have always felt this way, that this show of inter-faith discord is superficial. It is a way for politicians to seek votes; a way for orthodox institutions driven by faith to maintain their relevance in a globalised world where the only religion seems to be consumption. After all, the clergy too need to feed their families, and they like big cars and swanky mobiles and all the creature comforts.

During our discussion, the functionaries acknowledged that discord is part of the politics of perception. 'The party in power says that the appeasement of Muslims is a threat to the sovereignty of the nation. We say we're not a threat. But we're different. There are struggles outside the community and within it as well. But this external threat has cemented the bonds within the community,' one man said.

In that sense, the clerics are grateful to those in power. Politically, while the BJP is trying to polarise Hindu votes in their favour, they also end up polarising Muslim votes against them—a phenomenon clearly discernible in Deoband. The present government has helped Deoband reassert and re-establish its relevance in modern times. The polarisation of Muslim votes against the BJP is much stronger than that of Hindu votes in favour of them. According to the vote share of the 2014 Lok Sabha elections, when Narendra Modi won a clear majority for the BJP, at least half the Hindu population did not vote for the party. Hardly any Muslims voted for them.

However, Muslims are a sizeable political capital. Therefore, the government is trying to make inroads into the Muslim vote bank as well. The BJP needs the support, at least in part, of the country's largest religious minority. To this end, they make a distinction between 'good' Muslims and 'bad' Muslims. Sufis are 'good' Muslims, much to the ire of the orthodox Deobandis. This seems akin to the American classification, at one time, of the Taliban as good Taliban and bad Taliban, which had disastrous consequences. There has also been mounting international pressure: the Modi regime is increasingly seen as anti-Christian and anti-Muslim, not just pro-Hindu. And the blurring distinction between Hinduism and nationalism is disconcerting. The Prime Minister's Office (PMO) set the ball rolling in 2015 with a concerted effort to engage with a section of the Muslim population that is relatively amenable to their viewpoint. The subtext appeared to be: a good Muslim is one who rejects the dark shadow of violence and terrorism, and sees the noor or light in unity in diversity, multiculturalism and pluralism.

So, in June 2015, five months after he retired as the chief of the Intelligence Bureau, Syed Asif Ibrahim, a 1977 batch Indian Police Service officer, was appointed Special Envoy on Counter Terrorism and Extremism within the Prime Minister's Office (PMO), to report to the national security adviser, Ajit Doval. Ibrahim is an expert on terrorism and extremism.

Within a couple of months of his appointment, in August, a forty-four member delegation of the All India Ulama and Mashaikh Board (AIUMB)—founded ten years ago—led by its president, Syed Mohammad Kachhuchvi, met the prime minister in New Delhi. The delegation apprised Modi about a plan to organise an event to bring together exponents of Sufism from all over the world, to showcase Sufi art, culture, music and the philosophy of love and brotherhood that binds people together.

The question here is: was the AIUMB invited by the PMO, or did the AIUMB approach the PMO? When I met Kachhuchvi while reporting this story for the publication I worked for at that time, he explained to me in detail his dealings with the PMO. He had organised seven such events over the last ten years, all of which were local, with hardly any political patronage. He had approached many chief ministers and the prime minister for such patronage, but never got an encouraging response. Then, after the PMO got involved, everything changed. The AIUMB, a fairly unknown outfit with limited influence, suddenly had the support of the all-powerful PMO to organise the three-day-long World Sufi Forum, held between 17 and 20 March 2016. This was an event on an unprecedented scale, with delegates from twenty-two countries attending fourteen sessions in three days. Prime Minister Narendra Modi himself inaugurated the event at Vigyan Bhavan. When I asked Kachhuchvi about the specific role of Syed Asif Ibrahim in this event, he replied in Hindi: 'He is the pointsman in the PMO with whom we interacted on a regular basis. The visa issues and other aspects of organising an event of this scale cannot be managed without the help of the government. We interacted with Syed Asif Ibrahim in the PMO.' Kachhuchvi even got security cover.

AIUMB is an apolitical organisation and the World Sufi Forum was an apolitical event, Kachhuchvi maintained. If that was the case, why weren't representatives from other political parties invited? 'I didn't invite any political party, not even the BJP. I invited the prime minister of India,' he clarified.

The triple talaq legislation is also seen as direct interference in the affairs of the Muslims. Shortly after the Union Cabinet approved an ordinance on 19 September 2018, making the practice of instant talaq punishable, the All India Muslim Personal Law Board expressed its disapproval, stating that it was an interference in Muslim personal law. 'There is no doubt that the ordinance to make the practice of triple talaq a criminal offence is politically motivated,' Zafaryab Jilani, senior member of the All India Muslim Personal Law Board told the media.

'The practice of triple talaq has caused great injustice to Muslim women. The triple talaq has ruined the lives of many women and many are still living in fear,' Prime

Minister Modi announced from the ramparts of the Red Fort on Independence Day, 2018. He added, 'I assure my Muslim sisters and daughters that their rights will be protected, and the government will leave no effort to protect them. I promise and assure you that I will fulfil your aspirations.'

Muslims feel the ban on triple talaq is an infringement by the state in a religious matter. There is good reason for this feeling: a uniform civil code is not a fundamental right guaranteed by the Constitution of India, but only part of the directive principles of state policy listed elsewhere in the Constitution as desirable, but not mandatory, and not enforceable in the courts.

A fear psychosis is quietly being created amongst minorities, especially Muslims, who are projected as traitors in their own country. 'We have to swallow this insult every day,' said one of the librarian–clerics of Darul Uloom. And history is being employed very selectively to create a false impression about a whole community.

The government has failed Muslims: that may be true. But what have you done for your community? I asked the PRO. This question drew a mixed response. Some acknowledged that Muslims can't shun responsibility for the current state of affairs.

~

'Your time starts now,' the PRO said to Raul.

Raul started shooting like a commando as he walked briskly around the campus. The PRO, Aslam and a few others parked themselves in the middle of the field that was enclosed on all four sides by academic blocks, the administrative block and hostels. It looked like the main square of a medieval town. People were dressed in white salwar-kameez, women were conspicuously absent. Raul stood in the middle of the field and took long shots. His big zoom lens looked like the barrel of a gun. Scanning the surroundings, shooting non-stop, he proceeded towards the hostel. The PRO kept an eye on his watch while chatting with Aslam. I loitered, conscious of the pupils' reactions. They were uncomfortable. Some students went into their rooms. I walked through the corridors of the hostels. The students didn't encourage conversations. The curious stayed. They all had the same question: 'What's this photoshoot about?'

'A book,' I replied.

'These pictures will be used against us,' one of them said in a prophetic way. He was a skinny boy with a restless manner; his sharp-featured face was stern. Without waiting for a response, he turned and walked into a room with the doors open, curtain fluttering in the cool breeze. I followed him into the room. He disappeared into a hall that had many, many beds. A few were occupied by students who were lying down and reading. Some peeped out of the window to watch Raul in action. No one spoke. One of them gave me an unwelcoming glare from behind his book. I walked out feeling they were older than their age, not open to change or anything new.

When Raul approached the hostel, some pupils standing outside started to go inside. The PRO and Aslam didn't budge. They stood there witnessing this growing unrest in the campus because of a jeans-clad intruder fervently taking pictures with his oversized camera.

In the corridors of the residential block, white clothes were hanging to dry on wires tied to the pillars. Spotless white clothes fluttered in the breeze like peace flags announcing the cessation of hostilities. It was a pleasant sight on a sunny winter afternoon.

Among the innumerable white kurtas, pajamas, salwars and vests, there was no underwear. That triggered a thought. Are the pupils prohibited from wearing underwear? Is this another fatwa? I made specific enquiries. There was no authoritative word on it. 'Perhaps, they don't dry underwear in the open,' Raul said.

We had a meal at a local restaurant where a young scholar joined us for a cup of tea. A small, thin man with clear eyes on a fair, conical face. 'We gave Gandhi the title of Mahatma,' he said, referring to Deoband. 'And see how we are treated now—as traitors.'

Another conversation ensued about how belittled Muslims feel in their own country, for their faith is suspected, they are suspected, their love for their country is also suspected. It is said that they provide safe haven to terrorists. And their customs, their way of life, the way they treat women is all subject to criticism.

'On the contrary, this is a place where faith makes people responsible. There's never been a demonstration or a rally or a protest here. Darul Uloom, for the last forty years, has been contributing to the literacy mission. We have done more work than the government,' the young scholar said.

Our visit ended amicably. As the winter sun faded away and the sky turned red, we had sweet paan at a kiosk on an intersection. This trip had reinforced our belief in the composite culture that is organic to this country. We were happy.

AGRA

GHAR VAPSI

All around the world, the Taj Mahal in Agra is emblematic of India. But BJP parliamentarians have a different take on the world-famous monument. For instance, Vinay Katiyar believes that the seventeenth-century Mughal monument should be converted into the 'Tej Mandir'. Since October 2017, he has been claiming, without revealing the source of his information, that the Taj Mahal had actually been a Shiv temple and 'there used to be a Shivalinga there which had water dripping on it from above. That linga was removed and a mausoleum was built there'.

Chief Minister Yogi Adityanath of Uttar Pradesh also objects to this monument in the state he governs. In the past, he said that he was unhappy that a replica of the Taj Mahal is always presented to visiting foreign dignitaries. The Taj Mahal, in his view, is not a true symbol of Indian heritage. After widespread criticism of his remarks, he came up with a clarification that asserted a sort of ownership. He explained that there was no need to go into why and who built the Taj Mahal. 'What's important is that the Taj Mahal was built with the blood and sweat of the Indian labourers, the sons of Bharat Mata.'

Agra was the Mughal Empire's capital for a long time. It now is a crowded city that local authorities have tried and failed for decades to make neat and clean, even though it is a global tourist destination. A backpacker in Agra once described the Taj to me as, 'A lotus in a muddy pond, which is such an Indian thing.' The city of Agra is the 'muddy pond'. Unless things change. One of Prime Minister Narendra Modi's pet projects, the Swachh Bharat Mission launched on Gandhi Jayanti in 2014, aims to achieve a 'Clean India' by 2 October 2019. Yet, well past that deadline, Agra is a fine example of 'unclean India'.

Despite the squalor of the city, the Taj Mahal is the highest foreign exchange-earning monument in India, and the credit for this goes squarely to the long-dead Mughal emperor Shah Jahan. Hindus and Muslims have coexisted here for centuries without much of a problem, just as they have in most other Indian cities. But the tension is growing now. Lumpen elements, emboldened since 2014, are not happy with the way 'others' lead their lives. They do not like the relationship of these 'others' with their God.

The RSS–VHP agenda on this issue is fairly simple. All Muslims were Hindus at one point in time, they say. The logic goes like this: before the Prophet Muhammad was born in the sixth century, there was no Muslim on the planet. The same logic applies to other religions: before Christ, there weren't any Christians either. But Hinduism does not fit in easily with this logic of convenience. It's not even a religion, according to the Supreme Court of India. Hinduism is a way of life, and a fairly amorphous, flexible, tolerant and varied way at that. It is practiced in various ways in different parts of the country. For instance, wedding ceremonies differ every hundred kilometres, just as dialects do in the Hindi heartland.

Speaking in Agartala in December 2017, Mohan Bhagwat, the RSS chief, tried to simplify matters in case there was confusion. 'Anybody living in India is a Hindu,' he said. 'The Muslims in India are also Hindus.' He clarified that Hindutva is different from Hinduism. The meaning of Hindutva, he said, is to unite all communities.

In practical terms, Hindutva supporters have introduced something akin to a caste system amongst Muslims, differentiating between the in-house converts and the original imported Muslims. The former, they believe, are not a big problem. They are simply misguided and could make a course correction via reconversion. What is the point of inflexion, I wonder. Is a Muslim of three or four or five generations still a Hindu, and therefore, ideal for reconversion?

~

Next to a congested Hindu-dominated locality in Agra called Ved Nagari, there is a vacant plot of land where some three hundred and eighty-three Muslims reside, three hundred and fifty of whom are adults, in makeshift shacks of rags. They are not from Agra. They speak with each other in Bengali, and when they speak to the citizens of Agra, it is in Hindi with an unmistakable Bengali accent. They are the poorest of the poor, and illiterate. They deal in garbage, making a living from waste and recycling rags. Work starts before the break of dawn when they walk the city, collect waste, segregate it and deliver it to the recycling industry, making one hundred and fifty to two hundred rupees a day. They are done with the job by noon. They appeared to be a happy bunch of people, living together as a community. I had a feeling that grimness was a luxury they could not afford.

In December 2014, however, they were in major trouble. They were in the news for having converted back to Hinduism en masse—sixty families of them. *'Subah ka bhula agar shaam ko ghar aa jaye toh usse bhula nahi kehte'*, goes an old saying in Hindi, meaning, if a wayward friend or relative is ready to make amends for past mistakes, they should be welcomed back. This is a lovely idea. In theory, not always in the execution.

In Agra, an outfit by the name of Dharm Jagran Samiti (DJS), an affiliate of the RSS and VHP, is active when it comes to issues like love jihad. They actualised 'ghar vapsi', or homecoming, by converting the Bengali-speaking Muslim ragpickers of Ved Nagari to Hinduism.

Ajju Chauhan, a Bajrang Dal member, approached Ismail, the leader of this community of ragpickers—called thekedar (a Hindi word for contractor)—and made him lofty promises. When I heard this story, I was reminded of the famous quote from *The Godfather* by Mario Puzo: 'I'm gonna make him an offer he can't refuse.'

The ragpickers were offered a life of dignity. They were assured assistance with acquiring identity documents such as ration cards, Aadhaar numbers and so on, that would make them bona fide citizens of the world's biggest democracy. In this way, they would have access to various welfare schemes for the poor, perhaps even a pakka house. Suddenly, even their wildest aspirations seemed possible. They were asked to put their thumb prints on sheets of blank paper and they did it readily.

The next day, they were invited to a religious ceremony. This, they were told, was a 'bhumipujan', the worshipping of land before the commencement of a project, and they would be required to participate. They were encouraged to wear their skull caps during the ceremony, and so, they stood out in the crowd as Muslims attending a Hindu ceremony. Some of them were so poor that they didn't even have a skull cap, so they begged and borrowed one and participated in the havan, a quintessentially Hindu ritual.

It was an excellent photo-opportunity. Dozens of clearly distinguishable Muslims participating in a Hindu religious ceremony in the city of Agra, the capital of the Mughal empire that had ruled India for centuries. Many pictures were taken. The next day, these pictures were published in the leading dailies of northern India, with the claim that three hundred Muslims had converted back to Hinduism. Ghar vapsi is a reality, the media said. It is happening, and more and more people will reconvert to Hinduism. The DJS took the credit for this. It seemed like a historic moment for the resurgence of Hinduism in Hindustan.

That day, when Ismail returned home after his morning routine of ragpicking, he halted at a local paan shop where he was confronted with an existential question. 'Have you become Hindu?'

'No,' he laughed, for he thought it was a joke. An ugly joke, but nevertheless, a joke. He was accustomed to being judged because of his faith; it is almost an occupational hazard for a poor Muslim. But the paanwalla wasn't joking. He explained to Ismail, 'Your picture is in the newspapers. The paper says that not just you but all of you have reconverted to Hinduism.'

This was a rude shock for Ismail. He had a strong sense of disbelief. This was dhoka—treachery of the worst kind. To him, an assault on his faith was worse than being stabbed in the back. The poor are unwanted and an eyesore, but they are believers. Faith keeps them going under trying conditions. Ismail was beyond miserable. A part of him had been cut off. 'They did this to us because we are poor,' he told his community of ragpickers. He showed them the newspaper and told them what was written.

It took a while for this piece of information to sink in. When the ragpickers understood what had happened, they huddled together and cried. They do need a home. They do need papers that will give them the right to live in India as its own citizens. They do need to secure the futures of their children. They do need to lead a life worth living. But not at the cost of their faith. Faith is dearer to them than their lives. They were not willing to make this compromise. Faith is not a compromise. And tears are not signs of weakness. It was anger that brimmed from their eyes. They decided to fight back. They approached local Muslim clerics, sought their help and registered their protest.

The Uttar Pradesh Minorities Commission sent a four-member team to Agra and Aligarh to investigate. Three months later, its report said that the sixty families who allegedly converted to Hinduism are still Muslim. These families, according to the report, were mostly from West Bengal and Bihar and belonged to the poorer sections of the society. They were promised houses and made to sit near a 'havan kund'. The event was later propagated as religious conversion, the report stated. Now, the bluff was known to the world. The ghar vapsi had actually been cheap trickery.

~

The convincing of Muslims and Christians to 'return' to Hinduism is a bit like a marketing project, we learned. Teams are assigned tasks and targets. The young volunteers of DJS were forthright about what they needed to do in this, their service to the nation.

Reconversion is like changing the purpose of land use. For instance, to convert a particular piece of land earmarked for residential purposes to commercial use, a certain fee must be paid to the authorities. Similarly, there's a price attached to converting a Muslim to Hinduism. Allegedly, it costs a lakh to convert a Muslim, and forty thousand rupees to convert a Christian. So converting three hundred adult Muslims to Hinduism means that someone with very deep pockets supports this cause.

This particular case of conversion was a scam. Many Muslim clerics, including Mohammad Mudiseer Khan, the secretary of Tanzeem Ulama-e-Islam, raised the issue with the district authorities. The then district magistrate, Pankaj Kumar, assured them that justice would be done. An FIR was registered under Section 153B, 415B of IPC and some members of the DJS were put behind bars, including Ajju Chauhan.

Reports of ghar vapsi have come in from various parts of the country, with both Muslims and Christians as targets. Christian schools in Aligarh, Agra's neighbouring district, have been warned against celebrating Christmas with toys and gifts as it 'might lure students to Christianity'. This was said by Sonu Savita, the district president of the Hindu Jagran Manch, which is affiliated to the Hindu Yuva Vahini, an organisation founded by Chief Minister Yogi Adityanath.

Open Doors, a global charity that monitors the treatment of Christians worldwide, pointed out in a report that in the first six months of 2017, there were four hundred and ten attacks on Indian Christians—a substantial rise compared to previous years. In April 2016, in Gorakhpur—the district that sent Adityanath to Parliament four times—the police stopped a prayer meeting at a church that was being attended by approximately one hundred and fifty people, including eleven American tourists, after the Hindu Yuva Vahini complained that the event was a cover for religious conversion.

Meanwhile, in Agra, the same Muslim ragpickers, who had been welcomed into the fold of Hinduism, were now declared by the DJS to be outlaws—illegal immigrants from Bangladesh. The DJS reported the ragpickers to the authorities, demanding their dispatch to Bangladesh at the earliest. The message was clear: either, become a Hindu, or you don't even belong in this country and have no right to live in India.

The demagogue BJP MP Vinay Katiyar has been reiterating this message, time and again. In 2017, for instance, as reported by ANI, Katiyar, while referring to the Partition of India, said, 'Muslims should not be living in this country at all. When they divided the country on the basis of their population, what is the need for them to remain in India?'

A vicious campaign was initiated against these poor ragpickers. They were declared a potential security risk.

Once again, certain sections of the media played along; those who have willingly become government propagandists, feeding on scraps thrown to them by the demagogues of bigotry. This becomes evident when you actually meet the people involved and find a big disconnect between what was reported and what actually happened.

∼

The ragpickers were so scared that they packed their bags and vanished from Ved Nagari. Some left the city, some the country, and a few settled in a part of the city that fades into the hinterland. They live by a highway in a low-lying plot of land almost hidden from view.

Mohammad Mudiseer Khan did not take our calls for two days. We had to request some local journalists to persuade him to meet us. He invited us to his newly built house not far from where we were staying near Pacific Mall. When we got there, he was seated in a windowless room that opened into a corridor. The corridor led to a tall iron gate to the house, which was surrounded by a high wall. His home looked like a little fortress, standing alone in a big plot of barren land with no immediate neighbours. Khan runs many madrassas in Agra, where science, the arts and commerce are also taught.

He was seated at the far end of a double bed, with his legs folded beneath him. A polite gentleman, Khan is stout, bearded, middle-aged, perceptive and apprehensive. He talked slowly and carefully. He opened up to us after his initial hesitation, insisting we have tea and biscuits as he explained his predicament. Anything he says will be used against him, he said. These are testing times, and a wise man lies low and speaks little.

He clarified that he has severed all connections with the ragpickers; he hasn't had anything to do with them for years now, and he hasn't even met any of them for over a year. He was against them being fooled into converting to Hinduism, but if they're Bangladeshi, the law will take its own course. The matter needs to be investigated, their antecedents verified, and if they are illegal immigrants, they should be sent back. 'I'm not here to support illegal immigrants,' he said. Evidently, he doesn't want to fight the wrong battles.

After some persuasion, he instructed his son, fresh out of college, to take us to the ragpickers' new camp. An hour-long drive through the dust and din of Agra took us there. Khan's son's presence made the ragpickers comfortable enough to talk to us. They have good reason to be wary of strangers. Some entice them with the good things of life, others carry cameras and notebooks, and they all stab them in the back.

The ragpickers live in a depressed plot of land, like a huge, dry pit, a couple of metres below the level of the road that separates them from an orchard. The enclave seems to glow in the bright winter sun. Three rows of hutments run parallel to each other, with some twenty shacks in each row. The walls and roofs are made of tarpaulin held together with bamboo sticks. Mud embankments form the base of the tarpaulin walls and prevent water from seeping in. There is not a blade of grass. Instead, loose, dry and warm dust layers the ground. To enter a hut, you need to crawl. Inside, there's a layer of old bedsheets and sarees on the ground. The hut is dingy, dark and dungeon-like, but very cool.

The families' articles of daily use are meticulously arranged on wooden planks that rest on shaky bricks; stainless steel utensils are neatly lined up and glimmer in the torch light. Some families cook inside, but it's risky in these tarpaulin tinderboxes. There have been fire incidents in the past, some casualties as well. But the ragpickers continue to live dangerously. They have no choice. Women were sitting in front of their shacks, washing clothes and utensils and bathing their children. Some men were lying face down on mats, soaking in the sun. The waste they had collected lay segregated in big piles. There was a pile of old shoes—soles fetch good money. Plastic, beer bottles, rags, ropes, scrap, nuts and bolts, broken chairs, old bags, old clothes—everything is neatly arranged and segregated both inside the shacks and outside. No one pilfers from another's piles. They seem to remember each and every piece of waste and to whom it belongs. They express no bitterness about what had happened, but are nevertheless cautious.

Twenty-year-old Raja, scraggy, with a short frame and sparkling eyes, guided us around the area. He was a good listener and a glib talker, with a zest for the good things of life. He wore tight jeans and a tee-shirt that defined his skinny frame.

Most of the shacks in this place have wooden doors set in the tarpaulin walls. Some of these doors have been locked for months. The owners of these shacks have left, but the others keep their spaces. They might come back.

There was a strong sense of solidarity that made this camp a commune. The people share their joys and sorrows. This keeps them going in the face of uncertainty. They know that they are not welcome elsewhere. This ragpickers' colony lives on waste. It survives on scraps. Yet, the people here seem happy.

Raja held a little girl in his lap, a chubby toddler, granddaughter of the camp's oldest resident, Sufiya Begum. Though he is not related to the child, Raja played with her as if he were her uncle. The little girl made him pine for a 'little family' of his own, he said. But that would require harder work. Raja loves his freedom. He's not sure if he's ready for the responsibility of a family.

At the far end of the rows of shacks were two bathrooms—pits dug deep into the earth and covered with tarpaulin. One was being used, the other was abandoned. Dirty water stagnated in the drains, looking like deep scars filled with pus on the face of the dry earth. Flies and a foul smell hung in the air, which meant that people avoided spending any longer than necessary here.

Beyond the bathrooms was an open field at the far end of which was a motor-repair garage. Next to it was parked a rusting truck without tyres, resting on bricks. That's where the landlord lives. They don't like him, he's mercenary in his approach. 'He looks like a pauper,' Raja said, 'Though he's very rich.' He arrived at the colony, enquiring about our unscheduled visit.

The ragpickers live a methodical life. They go to work twice a day for three hours at a time, before sunrise and before sunset. Raja is not regular though. He's distracted, wants to marry, have kids of his own. He's fond of music and played us his favourite song on his mobile. Unlike many in his commune, he's open to outside influences. He has friends outside his closely-knit community. A barber and a college dropout—the latter, a Hindu—are two of his best friends. He often accompanies them to a movie. 'People are nice if you're nice to them,' he said.

At the age of sixty-two, Sufiya Begum is the most senior amongst the hundred residents. Ismail was no longer the thekedar, in fact, he was not even there and no one knew where he was. 'We have a new thekedar,' Raja's friend said. The new thekedar deals with the police and the authorities on behalf of the rest; he's docile and less of a leader than Ismail was. They miss Ismail, they said, and consider his successor a bit of a compromise candidate. The thekedar is relatively richer, and occupies the biggest shack.

The real power, however, rests with Sufiya Begum, the matriarch. She was their spokesperson because she has seen more of life than the others and is good at dealing with the local authorities, shedding tears and getting hysterical when confronted by cops. She is wise, we were told. She doesn't let people speak but only talks, and has the memory of an elephant. Skinny, tall but bent, her gait is swift and she smells of hair oil. She retired from ragpicking years ago, and is now being taken care of by the rest, looking after her granddaughter and playing ombudsman in case of a dispute. Sufiya Begum has outlived all her contemporaries. Ragpickers usually die early, for they are exposed to waste and arsenic throughout their lives. They handle toxic material without gloves, which contaminates the blood.

Sitting on a plastic chair, Sufiya Begum told us about her life. In the last forty years, she said, she had lived all over the country and had now been in Agra for seven years. Speaking in a Hindi that was almost indistinguishable from Bengali, she reminded me of the West Bengal chief minister,

Mamata Banerjee. It was difficult to follow what she was saying without Raja's translation, but we understood at least one thing. 'We were always Muslim. We are Muslim. We will die Muslim. It is better to die than to convert,' she said. Poverty makes these ragpickers desperate, but there are things in their life that are non-negotiable. Their faith is one of them.

KAIRANA

THE HINDU EXODUS

Before 2014, few people had heard of Kairana, a small, dusty, Muslim-dominated town in Shamli district in western Uttar Pradesh. There was no reason that this hamlet with its nearly 80 per cent Muslim population should have been in the news. It had even remained peaceful during the communal riots of 2013 in the neighbouring town of Muzaffarnagar. But then, it hit the headlines for all the wrong reasons. A year or so later, we set off on a sunny winter morning from Meerut to take a look around Kairana.

A busy main street was crammed with traffic. This commotion is normal in the Hindi heartland, where the streets are a stage for people. Since this is a small town, most cars on these streets are familiar to the residents, especially the shopkeepers. And everyone has a reputation to defend.

People were yelling and howling indiscriminately at each other, honking their horns and venting their pent-up anger at no one in particular but everyone in general. Honking, in my opinion, is a societal manifestation of the ego, of the patriarchal set-up and feudalistic mindset. All the drivers want to ensure that they get to negotiate the traffic first while others wait. It is a sort of entitlement that anyone in a big car wants pedestrians and cyclists to respect. Each car owner is a very important person, and he is keen to communicate this to others. Problems arise when there are many such people on the street at the same time.

They don't move, so no one moves. They want others to make way for them. Some have installed police sirens in their vehicles; others have a party flag fluttering on the bonnet. They only drive forward. The lesser mortals who constitute the crowd on the street must, like pests, get out of their way. The most privileged are the ones in big SUVs sporting the flag of the political party in power. They honk loudly and incessantly when stuck in the clamour, their disdain for others clear. Everyone makes way for the cars with a flag.

We had no flag on the bonnet of our ageing black Volkswagen Polo, and therefore, were stuck in this avoidable traffic snarl. I felt guilty, for Raul did most of the driving. Thankfully, we had nearly reached. Raul parked the car in front of a wide two-storied building that sat on the pavement like an eagle with its wings spread, overlooking the congested street where the social drama of hierarchies and entitlement was playing out. Across the street was a police station housed in an old cottage-like structure, flanked by residential and commercial complexes on both sides.

Hawkers and peddlers had lined up on both sides of the street, selling vegetables and fruits from carts the size of a bed clamped on four cycle wheels. On the ground floor of the building where we had parked were many eateries, with flies buzzing over uncovered sweets. We took a narrow flight of stairs up to the second floor. The room on the extreme right was the office of the Journalist Collective. Journalist Collective is an informal group of local journalists, mostly freelancers, struggling to make ends meet but with big aspirations. They have entered into an understanding to share information and avoid one-upmanship as much as possible. They include both Hindus and Muslims; some are reporters, others photographers. Each is committed to his professed belief system. But that does not affect their inter-personal relationships, or indeed their work, partnerships or friendships.

Arif, one of the collective's office bearers, was seated behind a big desk similar to that of a block development officer. People with ambitions in India's hinterlands arrange their work spaces to look like the office of a senior government functionary. Four other journalists were seated on a bench in front of a window, and they amicably discussed the alleged exodus of Hindus from Kairana with us.

They all had a public position about what took place in Kairana. Some claimed to be witnesses, but their descriptions varied. Two of them, one middle-aged, one fairly young, might have been members of the Vishwa Hindu Parishad. But their worldviews didn't hamper their day-to-day dealings with each other. They were tolerant of each other's views, which was heartening.

The loyalties of the smarter freelancers depend on which publication they are filing for. The suitability of news is more important than the authenticity of it. However, they are not entirely to be blamed for this mess. The journalists provide information almost as raw material, and do so while operating on a shoestring budget. A local photojournalist, for instance, gets five hundred rupees per photograph, but only if it's published. So they supply news, information and pictures selectively, carefully calibrated to the ideological leaning and political bias of the publication they are reporting for. They are acutely aware of the kind of stories that will be published and those that will never see the light of day. Thus, they don't bother to document things that will not be carried in a newspaper they are reporting for.

The media has a role to play when communal passions flare, resulting in tension, fear and uncertainty. The now deceased BJP MP of the region, Hukum Singh, claimed that three hundred and forty-six Hindu families had been forced to flee Kairana due to 'threats and extortion by criminal elements belonging to a particular community'. This was in 2016, when the state was preparing for the assembly elections. He furnished a list of Hindu families who had 'escaped' Kairana ('*Kairana se palayan karne wale Hindu pariwaron ki soochi*') due to growing communal hatred among the majority community—which happened to be Muslim in this small town.

This was a serious matter. Kairana could not be allowed to become another Kashmir. The National Human Rights Commission (NHRC) ordered the UP government to institute an enquiry. A few months later, as the enquiry was under way, Hukum Singh, an accused in the Muzaffarnagar riots case, shifted his stand. The reason for the exodus was 'not communal' but due to the poor law and order situation in the region, he said. He then furnished another list of families who had left the neighbouring city of Kandhla: *'Kandhla se palayan karne wale pariwaron ki soochi'*. The word 'Hindu' was conspicuously absent in the title of the list from Kandhla. There was no communal connotation to this exodus.

Expectedly, the BJP promised in its election manifesto for the 2017 state assembly polls, a special department in every district to stop mass migration because of communal tension.

In the meantime, the NHRC enquiry conducted by a four-member team comprising Deputy Superintendent of Police Ravi Singh and Inspectors Suman Kumari, Saroj Tiwari and Arun Kumar found that that over two hundred and fifty Hindu families had indeed left Kairana due to the fear of the members of a particular community that was 'in the majority in the area'. The abysmal law and order situation, according to the fact-finding enquiry, was due to the dominance of the Mukim Kala gang in the region. 'The notorious gang leader Mukim Kala had committed at least forty-seven cases of robbery, murder, dacoity, extortion and violation of the Arms Act during a span of just five years between 2010 and 2015, in the states of UP, Haryana and Uttarakhand,' the report stated.

When Yogi Adityanath came to power, he ordered strict action against the gangsters in a bid to liquidate the 'mafia raj' in the state and replace it with, as it is popularly referred to, 'Yogi raj'. Some of those alleged gangsters were dreaded criminals, outlaws and people with criminal records, no doubt. But the fact of the matter is that everyone killed in the police encounters was Muslim.

The government of the day has much of its day-to-day dealings with citizens through police. It has become the most crucial interface between the state and its subjects. The popular narrative was that the exodus of Hindus in Kairana had been caused by the fear of the primarily Muslim mafia and extortionists. Asif, a local journalist, showed us gory pictures of people gunned down in cold blood by the police on charges of being gangsters—one of them shot through his head at point-blank range, his eyes open, mouth agape as if death had come as a surprise. Or perhaps, he died before he realised he'd be dead meat.

Kairana is not the only place in Uttar Pradesh where encounter attacks are being carried out in the name of fighting criminals and the mafia. This has been the most terrifying aspect of the so-called 'Yogi raj' all across the state. Till January 2018, according to the state government's figures, one thousand and thirty-eight 'encounters' had been carried out, killing a total of forty-four people and leaving two hundred and thirty-eight injured. In the process, the security forces—read police—suffered four casualties in the entire state. Unofficial figures, which are of course a matter of speculation but can be more representative of the ground reality, put the number of encounters at fourteen hundred. So far. As a result, 'The NHRC has taken suo motu cognisance of media reports about the government of Uttar Pradesh allegedly endorsing killings in encounters by police, seeking improvement in the law and order situation in the state,' the commission said in a statement in November 2017, giving the UP government three weeks to respond.

Around the same time, on 20 November 2017, Yogi Adityanath, as reported by the Press Trust of India, brought

The veiled woman is a resident of the ragpickers' hamlet in Agra. Their community exists on the margins of the society, almost hidden from view. They clear the city of its garbage, segregate it, fuel the recycling industry, and make a living out of waste management. They are quite poor but faith keeps them going, and they are not ready to barter it for monetary gain.

Sufiya Begum, 62, is the oldest resident in the ragpickers' colony.

In Agra, passengers share an auto rickshaw, irrespective of caste or creed.

Women in colourful burqas in Kairana. A town of vibrant colours, Kairana has now been given a communal shade after news of the alleged forced exodus of Hindus was spread.

A woman walks down the street in Kairana.

up the issue of the Hindu 'exodus' from Kairana while he campaigned for urban local body polls in the state. He assured people that the rule of law would prevail in the state and 'Kairana-like' incidents would not happen again. *'Kanoon ke raaj ke aadhar par hum logon ne tai kiya ki aaj pradesh ke andar Kairana jaisi ghatnaon ki punaravritti nahi ho sakti* (On the basis of law, we have decided that Kairana-like incidents won't be allowed to happen again),' the Lucknow edition of the *Indian Express* quoted Adityanath.

~

We hired a local scribe from the Journalist Collective to help us do our own fact-finding. He seemed to know everyone who mattered. Kairana is a small place; people know each other. As we met more and more people, congenial but guarded, we found no signs of an exodus of Hindus for the reasons reported. But there was tension in the air and people were sceptical about the relationship between the two communities.

We must have met a dozen families, both Hindus and Muslims, and none of them disputed the fact that people had moved out of Kairana. But it was not because Muslims were gunning for Hindus. They left due to the lack of employment opportunities. The law and order situation also had a bad impact on the local economy.

Our first destination was a madrassa not far from where we had parked our car. A side lane took us to an arched gateway that opened into a big courtyard. The courtyard was flanked on all three sides by a double-storied building that housed classrooms. A new multi-storied wing was being constructed on one side to accommodate more students.

The pupils were dressed in white ankle-length salwar-kameez and skull caps. They were filled with nervous energy. Not just because they were young and boisterous, but also because two strangers in jeans and t-shirts had just walked in, one of whom held a camera and the other was insisting on speaking to the principal. When a stranger enters, every student and teacher in the madrassa seems to know instantly. They worry. Who are they? Why are they here? What do they want?

Some of the older students in their late teens remembered the 2013 communal riots only too well. They were peeping out of the windows with nervous excitement in their eyes. There is a lack of trust—a justified reaction when the government of the day is perceived as communally motivated.

I thought about this suspicion, this feeling of being besieged that Muslims in India feel today, while looking into the eyes of the pupils looking out of the windows of the first floor. These students are the next generation of India. What are they experiencing in their formative years? This madrassa was converted into a refugee camp during the Muzaffarnagar riots in 2013. Dozens of Muslim families lived here for more than a month. There was uncertainty and danger. No one felt safe, even here in Kairana, a Muslim-majority town.

Munawwar, a young man with a skinny frame and mild-mannered, is the principal of the madrassa. We met him in the courtyard and he escorted us to his office, an empty room with red carpets to sit on. There were old bookshelves filled with even older scriptures, a small desk, some loose papers, and an open door that allowed the afternoon sun to fill the room. He offered us tea but politely declined to talk. Anything said or unsaid would be construed against him and his institution. He feels watched and judged by the authorities, as if they are waiting for him to make a mistake. In the eyes of the state, Muslims believe, every Muslim is a potential miscreant. And so they go out of their way to demonstrate that they are not miscreants, but well-meaning, responsible citizens of this country. The best way to do this is by keeping their mouths shut.

We wandered around the old city to verify the reported cases of Hindu exodus. It was a happy place for walkers. Raul was fascinated by the Bohra burqa. The women here are imaginative, even experimental, in the burqas they wear. They are colourful and the cut is different. Some burqas looked like robes with frills, some had elaborate embroidery. The top of the burqa rests on the head like a skull cap, unlike the more common veil-like design that covers the face.

The houses on either side of the narrow lanes embraced each other. The local journalist accompanying us escorted us to the houses of people who had reportedly left the city out of fear of the Muslim majority. When we knocked on their locked doors, neighbours came out to see what was happening. At one place, we were mobbed. There were a dozen people around us, all of them wanting to talk. They told us that the locked houses belong to people who don't live here, but that those people haven't left the city for good. They work elsewhere and return often to check on their property. The neighbours are vigilant and keep their property safe for them. They were disturbed by our pointed enquiries and suspicious of what we would write and the consequences of it.

If you meet a few people randomly, whether Hindu or Muslim, it is soon clear why some people left the town. The reasons were not communal but economic; it was a search for better opportunities elsewhere as many Muslim-owned houses have remained locked for years like those of the Hindus. Local estimates vary; some say one hundred, others say close to one hundred and fifty Muslim families have also migrated out of the city in search of a better life and security. Gangsters and extortionists don't discriminate between Hindus and Muslims. The neighbours listed many instances where Muslim families were pestered by lumpen elements. The so-called exodus was more a failure of the law and order machinery than anything else.

A retired Muslim teacher who asked us not to use his name, told the story of his brother who migrated to Delhi seven years ago. Three rooms in his house have remained locked ever since. The brother rarely visits Kairana.

We verified that some of the people who were said to have been part of the Hindu 'exodus' had actually migrated years ago due to lack of opportunities, not because they had been hounded out. Their houses were intact, rusted locks dangled on the doors, and the neighbours, mostly Muslims, guarded their homes for them.

Back on the street, as we walked to a local vegetable market, Raul's camera attracted a lot of attention. Children wanted to examine it and have a few pictures taken. Middle-aged men were curious about what had brought us to this little town. They don't trust journalists and the narrative we were planning to weave was a matter of general concern. The older people were not just anxious, but a shade angry.

'Why are you taking pictures?' asked an old, clean-shaven man in a loose, somewhat soiled, kurta-pajama. He felt unsafe, as if we were walking around with guns in our hands. His little town had become a spectacle for the whole country; he hated it. He had nothing to hide, but there was nothing to demonstrate either. This old man just wanted the people of his little town to be left alone. Their miseries were not just another juicy story.

Whether Muslim or Hindu, everyone struggled with unemployment. Unemployment leads to resentment; some young men look for easy money, and crime is attractive. This is not a communal issue and gunning down Muslim outlaws in the region is not a solution either. This city had been treated—like every Muslim-dominated pocket of the country—as a breeding ground of terror and melting pot of insurgencies, even before Yogi came to power. They are tired of being judged.

On the day we visited, the people were pouring out on the streets, wearing their best attire, to attend the fair that had been organised after a gap of several years. A big Ferris wheel and a giant swing were visible even from where we stood.

We crossed from the old city, which is a Muslim-dominated area, to a newly developed locality called Teacher's Colony, where mostly Hindus reside. This seems to be a trend: the older, more cramped parts of the city are increasingly being occupied by Muslims, while Hindus reside in newer residential areas that have broad streets with street lights, large dwellings, parks and recreational centres, space to park vehicles, and all the other amenities of an easy life. There's also less load-shedding, if the locals are to be believed. It's hard to believe that this is a mere coincidence.

Teacher's Colony has well-paved roads with some grass and vegetation, clean but for stagnant, green water in a vacant plot, next to which a pig laboured at a pile of garbage. In this locality, we were looking for a man listed as having left Kairana because of intimidation by Muslim lumpen elements. That was not a fact. An older man standing at the entrance of another house had misguided us. He was a lean fellow of short stature, wearing a white lungi and an oversized shirt. His tone was impolite and his sunken cheeks trembled as he spoke louder than the situation demanded. Instead of answering our enquiries, he said in Hindi, 'All left because of gundagardi.'

'But why are you here then?' we asked.

'I'm afraid of no one,' he retorted. It was an aggressive assertion of how secure he felt.

He was wrong. Many people live here peacefully. And we did trace the person we were looking for, but he refused to talk to us and refused to be mentioned in the book by name. Some residents of Kairana had left years ago for bigger cities, to live in greener pastures. But that's the general trend in an India that is progressively becoming urbanised.

MATHURA

THE REAL GAU-RAKSHAK

It was already afternoon when we left Meerut for Mathura, confident that we would get to the Maan Mandir Sewa Sansthan ashram located on and around the Gahvar Van hill in Barsana, Mathura, by early evening at the latest. But we had been gloriously and overly optimistic. That the streets of small towns are an extension of its residents' personal space is a pan-Indian phenomenon. It has been said that, in this part of the country, public spaces are considered common areas and privacy is not valued very highly. Some may even argue that the people here believe that anything private is necessarily sinister. Therefore, older folks, no longer actively earning a living, keep an eye on what is happening around them. People always know what others in their neighbourhood are doing, what they eat and drink, who stayed awake till late hours, who came home late, who their visitors are and what time of the day they arrive.

So, a road here is like a backyard or a park, where people stroll and chat, eating groundnuts, littering their surroundings, playing cards, and doing a host of other things, religious, recreational and occupational. As a result, cars, scooters and cycles, cots and chairs, hawkers and peddlers, cows and pigs all seem to exist in some state of profound inactivity on the road. Only dogs are seemingly vigilant, running around, fending for themselves and guarding their territory. Like everyone else, they too feel a primal right to it.

This is not a laidback suburb, though, but Mathura: right by National Highway 2, which connects Delhi to Agra. Mathura, the land where Lord Krishna grew up and performed his youthful lilas, is a bit of a trap. At least it was a trap on that particular day, thanks to the traffic. Not even God can rescue a hapless traveller on this route.

All kinds of vehicles, big and small, two-three-four wheelers, compete for space with humungous trucks, each driver vigilant for the slightest opportunity to inch forward. In the process, all of them seem to merge at the crossings as though an invisible whirlpool were pulling them in from different directions. Everyone, rich and poor, Muslim and Hindu (the members of each community fairly distinctive in their attire, mannerisms and hairdo) is subject to the same lack of madness, the same chaos. In that sense, the Mathura crossing on National Highway 2 is an egalitarian space.

Is it true that smaller dogs bark louder? Because, on the road, it seems that the smaller the vehicle, the bigger the driver's ego. Motorcyclists are good at blocking, for instance, if they can't move forward, they won't let others move either. But, eventually, everyone finds ways to move forward, centimetre by centimetre, if not on the road then on the muddy service lane and the construction sites of long-proposed flyovers.

It was as if the hospitable Lord Krishna wouldn't let us leave his birthplace without spending some time there. Sadly, the divine land of Krishna is disputed. The Krishna Janmabhoomi temple in Mathura is believed to be located where a prison cell once stood—the jail cell where Lord Vishnu incarnated as baby Krishna. A heavy deployment of security forces now stands outside it. The Kashi Vishwanath temple in Varanasi has similar security arrangements. These temples are the most communally sensitive spots in the country because each shares a wall with a mosque. The Shahi Eidgah mosque is adjacent to the Krishna Janmabhoomi temple, while the Gyan Vapi mosque is next to the Kashi Vishwanath temple.

In July 2003, the VHP and its parent organisation, the RSS, passed a resolution in Kanyakumari, articulating their resolve not to give up their claim to the land where the Gyan Vapi mosque in Varanasi and the Eidgah in Mathura stand. The latter was built by the Mughal emperor Aurangzeb in 1669 at the spot where an ancient Govind Dev temple existed, claim the VHP and the RSS. Pravin Togadia, a rabble-rousing leader of the VHP, said that some thirty thousand mosques in India can be claimed by Hindus. The generous VHP is not asking for all of them, he declared.

By now, we had surrendered to the traffic. The car was hot despite the air-conditioning, but it still felt like a refuge from the dust cloud outside. We were not talking much today, and weren't moving fast enough.

When we were not stuck in traffic, we had to make frequent stops to ask for directions. People here are dangerously generous. They will help even if they aren't in a position to. They will helpfully misguide hapless travellers.

Yet, somehow, we were still heading towards our elusive destination.

The sun was precariously low on the horizon when we neared Barsana—in these parts, this time is called 'gau-dhuli bela', literally, the time when cows return after grazing, their hooves conjuring a cloud of dust over the landscape in the fading light of the day. The earthy smell of cow dung was all-pervasive. It was all quite picturesque.

The cow is a sacred, maternal figure that provides life-sustaining milk. Lord Krishna was a cowherd. Cow dung mixed with mud is used to plaster the walls and floors of rural households. The deity Kamadhenu brings contentment and is considered the mother of all cows. Depicted as a white cow with the wings of a bird, the tail of a peafowl, and the head of a woman, she contains thirty-three crore gods in her body.

We stopped at a diversion and asked two young men on a motorcycle parked next to a cigarette kiosk for directions. They provided us with detailed directions. Now that they knew where we were headed, they insisted that we give a lift to two older men who were heading broadly in the same direction and waiting at the kiosk for public transport.

We had decided that, as a matter of policy, we would not encourage hitchhiking. Our luggage, cameras and other equipment were scattered on the back seat of the car. We politely declined their forceful 'suggestion'. One of the two young men, bony-faced and thick-lipped, with a sharp nose and intent bulging eyes, examined the inside of the car through the windows. Though he seemed to be in his late twenties, he had little facial hair, wore several anklets, and had a piece of red cloth loosely wrapped around his long, thin neck. Once again, he insisted that we take the two older men in our car. It was not a request. We remained adamant and left without the two on board. They chased us on their bike as if we had run away with their wallets.

~

Barsana, the last town before Brahmaachal Parvat, was inaccessible to vehicles that evening. 'How can you forbid people from crossing a town?' I asked the potbellied and grubby cop who had been assigned the job of directing traffic away from the city. 'You can walk, but a car is not allowed,' he repeated.

'What if we have to take the car to the next town?'

'Go back and take the bypass,' he instructed. We complied.

The bypass was still under construction, smooth for most part, with mounds of mud on either side of the road. Some stretches were barely motorable, but we managed to negotiate them even though it felt as though we were sitting on a camel.

Lord Krishna was testing our resolve. It was Ekadashi, or the eleventh day of the month according to the Hindu calendar; an auspicious day. Hundreds of Hindus had gathered for a grand public ritual that was being performed inside the town. Though we weren't allowed in, we could participate—or rather, couldn't avoid participating— thanks to hundreds of loudspeakers blaring out the chants for everyone to hear. The people on the road were in no hurry, it seemed, to get anywhere.

When we reached the foot of the hill that hosts the Maan Mandir Sewa Sansthan, a sort of ennui had set in.

There were few people on the street as darkness descended on the muddy road that led to the ashram. We passed through the narrow lanes of the congested town of Gahvar Van. It seemed like a mini-Vrindavan, which, in turn, I've always thought of as a mini-Varanasi. These ancient pilgrimage towns have lots in common.

This was my second visit here in two years and I saw some significant changes. Part of the road that led to the ashram had been metalled and the rest was in different stages of construction.

We drove on tentatively. I had been in touch with Sunil Singh from the ashram all this while, informing him of our slow progress. He was glad it took us longer to get there than we had planned. That afternoon, he had been busy attending to some important visitors. A member of the state cabinet and the district magistrate of Mathura had been with him, planning the details of Chief Minister Yogi Adityanath's impending visit. The meeting had lasted several hours.

Uttar Pradesh is the most populous state in India, which fills eighty seats in Parliament. A third of all BJP members of Parliament are from this state. The state of UP was instrumental in making Narendra Modi the country's prime minister in 2014. Within the BJP and amongst mediapersons, Adityanath's popularity is next to Narendra Modi himself. That's not good enough for the chief minister.

He has always been open to challenges, from an early age, not just in his spiritual pursuits, but in his ability to galvanise people around the beliefs and convictions that shape his way of life. He was only twenty-seven years old in 1999 when he was first elected to the Lok Sabha from Gorakhpur. Since then, he has had four consecutive terms as a member of Parliament. He is also the head of the Gorakhnath Math.

In 2017, when he resigned from the Lok Sabha after becoming the chief minister of UP, Adityanath famously said in Hindi that he was a year younger than the then Congress President Rahul Gandhi and a year older than his predecessor in UP, Samajwadi Party President Akhilesh Yadav. He has demonstrated over and over that he is a cow-lover and that is why he has been an extremely proactive gau-rakshak, or cow-protector.

During his very first year in office, Adityanath announced several innovative schemes for the welfare of cows. In December 2017, he launched the concept of 'cow safaris' in at least twenty-four districts of Uttar Pradesh. Further, he said, the land recovered from the ongoing anti-encroachment drive in the state would be devoted to sanctuaries for stray cattle, primarily around the bigger cities, with a special emphasis on the Bundelkhand region. Further, it was proposed that fourteen dairies would be set up across the state of Uttar Pradesh. Adityanath made this announcement on the floor of the state assembly where the BJP rules—they won three hundred and twenty-five seats out of four hundred and three.

Needless to say, the government of Uttar Pradesh has already initiated a crackdown on illegal slaughterhouses across the state. Adityanath has time and again made it clear that beef consumption is illegal. For instance, at a function hosted by the VHP's Gauraksha Vibhag (cow-protection department), he said: 'If any person indulges in

cruelty to cows (let alone beef eating), he will find himself
behind bars.' Beef consumption and export are banned in
the state. 'When we are dependent on cows for milk, are
we not duty-bound to also care for and protect them?'
Adityanath asked all the beef eaters—read Muslims.

So, it was not surprising that he planned to visit Maan
Mandir Sewa Sansthan to draw inspiration for his own
cow-protection policy. Sunil Singh is thus a useful man to
the ruling dispensation.

~

Sunil Singh's car was following ours when he called me to
find out where we were.

'About to reach the ashram,' I replied.

'Are you in a black car?'

'Yes,' I said.

'I'm in the car behind you.'

Raul and I pulled over and he joined us in our car.

We exchanged pleasantries. He couldn't place me till he
saw me. I had visited the ashram a couple of years earlier
to do a story about how a certain segment of humanity is
the cow's biggest enemy. As we entered the ashram now,
illuminated by warm sodium lights under the red sky of
a dying day, our surroundings had an occult-like quality.
I wondered, is this a temple to the cow? For sure, it's a
retreat or an old-age home for cows. In a state of general
excitement, I began explaining to Sunil what science had
to say, that cows and dogs, followed by perhaps the horse,
were the earliest friends of mankind.

Sunil is a big guy with a stout, solid torso that supports
an enormous round, balding head. He looks like he might

have been a wrestler, though he has never wrestled. Sunil was barely five years old when he joined Ramesh Baba, the spiritual leader and founder of this ashram, in the late 1980s. Since then, he has been here, working day in and day out, and has risen through the ranks to become, for all practical purposes, the ashram's chief executive officer. He shares some of his management responsibilities with two other influential men deputed by Ramesh Baba.

Sunil's face glows in the fading light of the day. His menacing figure belies an affable disposition. He's a vegetarian and does not consume any mind-altering substances, not even tobacco. He has a certain reputation in the region. People know him, and those who know him revere him. It's the kind of reverence that's laced with more fear than love.

Particularly in the Hindi heartland, with its patriarchal, feudalistic traditions, it is muscle power and grit that keep a set-up like this running. Sunil is capable of defending the ashram; he's not dependent on the police like an ordinary citizen. The local cops treat him like a mafia man who can pull strings in the corridors of power. The chief minister of the day is eager to travel to the ashram to meet him and his guru, Ramesh Baba, who, Sunil informed us, was not well.

Sunil took us on a guided tour of the facility, which looked rather like the ranches of rich farmers abroad, I thought. Thousands of tonnes of pasturage and fodder were stored in piles the size of hills and sand dunes inside huge enclosures that looked like airplane hangars, separated from each other by muddy roads. Trucks plied intermittently on these roads leaving a trail of rising dust. There were dozens of men at work, loading and unloading the fodder. It's a mega exercise, feeding ninety thousand cattle—male, female and calves. This whole enterprise had been set up out of pure benevolence. Only twelve hundred of these ninety thousand cattle are milch cows; the rest are either well past their prime or are calves and bulls and, therefore, economically useless.

The cattle are housed in huge open enclosures that extend for acres, segregated according to their gender and age. Calves have a separate enclosure. The caste system originated from the segregation of humanity based on vocations and skills. The milch cows, the privileged ones, have a separate enclosure with a roof and are treated like Brahmins of the past.

The facility is well managed, and there are forward and backward linkages that make it an efficient enterprise. For instance, there's an in-house captive power plant that is fuelled by biogas produced by treating tonnes of cow dung on a daily basis.

From a vantage point on the hill, the dusty, flat landscape extends as far as the eye can see. And at the base of the hill, thousands of cows fill the countryside. From atop the hill, the whole compound looks like a giant ant colony.

It is not easy to run such a big establishment on charity. Sunil manages this complex operation with a simple philosophy. 'We started this place with only two cows in the year 2009, and within a year, we had about a thousand of them,' Sunil recalled. He had no idea that the initiative would become so big so fast. 'There will soon be one hundred thousand cows as their numbers are rising on a daily basis. How are we going to take care of so many cows?' he'd often asked Baba who wasn't perturbed at all. 'Baba told me prophetically, "As long as we utilise the money we receive for the upkeep of cows on the cows, there'll never be a shortage of resources,"' recollected Sunil. Sure enough, Ma Annapurna made money for the upkeep of the cows. 'Donations kept coming and we never diverted money meant for the cows and there was never a shortage,' Sunil said with a sparkle in his eyes.

Ramesh Baba, now in his eighties, was born into a Brahmin family. His father Baldev Prasad Shukla, also known as Shukla Bhagwan, retired as the deputy inspector general of police and was an amateur astrologer and palmist. He offered free consultations and his predictions were never wrong. Ramesh Baba was a bright student and a talented singer; he impressed the classical singer D.V. Paluskar. He could play several musical instruments, such as the pakhavaj, khol, mridangam, dholak and tabla.

Some sixty years ago, Baba came to Gahvar Van. It is believed that every tree here was planted by Radha, Krishna's consort. Baba started living in the Maan Mandir located at the top of Brahmaachal Parvat—believed to be the head of Brahma—though it was the hideout of a dacoit called Jahan Daku.

This former dacoit hideout is now a modern farmstead. As Sunil escorted us to the newly constructed 'main office', crickets stridulated like an orchestra in the backdrop. It was a musical sundown. The campus was engulfed in an eerie darkness. The main office is built on an elevated platform supported by pillars. Hundreds of cows live underneath it.

We took a flight of stairs, walked down a corridor and entered a guest room—a squarish hall with large windows and soiled curtains that had been drawn back. At the far end of the room was an oversized double bed, as though two king-sized beds had been joined together. The air in the room was stale. I made myself comfortable on a plastic chair while Sunil settled at the edge of the bed in front of me. We were offered organic tea, which wasn't tea at all. It was milk boiled with Arjuna saal (the bark of the Arjun tree which has great medicinal qualities), some herbs and a lot of sugar. It was sweet, tasty and energising.

We could see, in the cold light of the multiple tube lights, that Sunil's bulging eyes were red-rimmed. He hadn't slept for three days, he said. 'I can work for three more days,' he declared, even as he fought exhaustion. The bed seemed to wake his suppressed need for slumber. After a brief while and few sips of herbal tea, he initiated a hearty conversation.

∼

I had first met Sunil two years earlier while covering a story for the news magazine *Outlook*. The local police had suggested that I talk to him, but they had also warned me that, though he does commendable work in taking care of thousands of cows, he is a mafia man. This made sense: when things can't be explained, they are necessarily illegitimate. In this part of the world, acquiring illegitimate gains is not as difficult as retaining them. That requires muscle power. When I eventually met him, Sunil had brushed aside all the talk about a mafia connection as baseless allegations and we'd had a good conversation.

The situation is different now. There's a new regime. Adityanath is the chief minister. Legitimacy often has a lot to do with who's in power. These thoughts played in my head as we began chatting.

Sunil, it turned out, was not a diehard fan of Yogi Adityanath. It's not that Yogi Adityanath's cow vigilantism is not effective, he said. Gau-taskari or the smuggling of cows has come down. It is now 70 per cent of what it had been a year ago. But that means there are 30 per cent more cows on the streets in this region. Not that anyone notices it, for cows have always been around. You can't miss them as they eat garbage and plastic bags in the suburban landscape, or stand listlessly in the middle of the road as if their journey had ended just there. The piles of garbage, the snake charmers and the revered cows on the streets of India have, in fact, fascinated visitors since the times of Rudyard Kipling.

Sunil was not happy about the rise in the number of abandoned cows. There's a limit to how many cows he can accommodate in this ashram. They are abandoned like the widows of Vrindavan, left to fend for themselves when they are past their prime, just when they need to be cared for the most. They are sacred, mother-like, not to be killed for meat, but they are abandoned to starvation and disease. The inherent sacredness of a cow and the treatment it receives is typical of India, a country of glorious contradictions.

Sunil said that farmers are not happy with so many abandoned cows strolling around. They are everywhere, like pests, and they enter farms, trample on the crops and destroy them.

'It's a big problem here,' he said. Some farmers, mostly Hindu, are then forced to bring in people who are part of the supply chain of the tanneries in the neighbouring areas. Mathura's neighbouring district of Agra is a leather-industry hub.

There's an economic reason to discourage the rise in the number of stray cows. A dead cow is more lucrative than an untended cow. Sometimes, death is a respite. Sunil does not advocate killing the cows; he is simply concerned about the dignity of life of an animal that is sacred. There is a certain ecosystem that shouldn't be disturbed—the economy of cows. So, in a way, Sunil justifies the slaughter of cows, but he is dead against them being served at dinner.

Until recently, India was the biggest exporter of beef in the world. In 2015, India exported 2.4 million tonnes of beef and veal compared to 2 million tonnes by Brazil and 1.5 million by Australia. Together, these three countries accounted for nearly 60 per cent of global beef export; India alone accounted for about a quarter.

But, especially since 2014, people have been killed by cow vigilante groups if found in possession of cows or transporting them or eating beef, even if the nature of the meat was unverifiable. Many of those attacked, even killed by gau-rakshaks were Muslims. Recently, a migrant worker from West Bengal, Mohammad Afrazul, was hacked to death with a cleaver and then set on fire by an overzealous gau-rakshak in Rajsamand, Rajasthan.

This was not an isolated incident. Since 2014, Muslims and some Dalits have been attacked across the Hindi belt by cow vigilantes who seem to operate with impunity. Many of the states where such attacks are rampant have a BJP government. The Supreme Court issued notices to the governments of Rajasthan, Haryana and Uttar Pradesh in January 2018 for not following its order to take stern steps to stop the violence in the name of cow vigilantism. The bench headed by the then Chief Justice of India, Dipak Misra, with Justices A.M. Khanwilkar and D.Y. Chandrachud as members, observed that the cow vigilantes behave as though they are a 'law unto themselves' and issued directions that a 'senior police officer shall take prompt action and ensure (that) vigilante groups and such people are prosecuted with quiet promptitude'.

~

Two years ago, Sunil had told me that one or two cows are stolen every day. He carried out a bit of an investigation to learn who the culprits were. They were poor people, mostly Hindus. One of them, caught red-handed, was a Hindu boy in his late teens. He would sell the stolen cows across the border in Rajasthan for their hides. Each dead cow would fetch the locals at least a couple of thousand rupees—useful to run the household for a month or two.

This young boy was not handed over to the police. Instead, Sunil asked him, as reparation, to help in the construction of a local temple for a few months. Locals tend to carry out Sunil's decree without protest.

Two years later, his version has changed a bit. 'Both Hindus and Muslims steal cows,' he said, more democratic now about the religious identity of those who commit this crime. Though, both Muslims and Hindus commit the crime, they have different roles. Muslims kill the cows and Hindus facilitate the killing. The economic benefits come to Hindus as well because they are the traders, while Muslims do the dirty work. 'And of course, Hindus don't eat beef. They kill those who eat beef,' Sunil laughed. This was not funny.

He made some innovative suggestions that I'm sure he will communicate to Yogi Adityanath when he meets him

next. One such idea is a subsidy on cow dung. Cow dung
has been the main source of fuel for cooking in the Indian
hinterland for centuries. Every part of a cow, alive or dead,
is useful. Cow urine, for instance, has been found to be
beneficial in a host of medical conditions such as diabetes,
blood pressure, asthma, psoriasis and many more.

The father of the nation, Mahatma Gandhi, was
categorical about cow protection. To him, 'Mother cow'
was in many ways better than the 'mother who gave us
birth', and therefore, he said, 'Cow protection is the gift of
Hinduism to the world' and 'Hinduism will live so long as
there are Hindus to protect the cow'. Gandhi had a message
which is now relevant for the lumpen cow vigilante groups,
who don't protect cows and kill humans. Gandhi had
said: 'I would not kill a human being for the protection
of a cow, as I will not kill a cow to save a human life, be
it ever so precious.' In other words, the life of a cow is as
valuable as that of a human being, but this should not lead
to bloodshed.

'No politician has done anything for the cow,' Sunil
said in Hindi. 'They only do lip service, but there is nothing
on the ground. Akhilesh Yadav did nothing, neither has
Yogi.' And then, he added after a long pause, '*Ab tak* (so
far).'

Because there is no sincerity in the way cows are
treated, there is a general decline in all spheres of life, Sunil
pointed out, particularly the environment. The Yamuna is
polluted. The natural systems are contaminated. People are
dying early; hepatitis B is on the rise. Something is wrong,
he said, sounding impassioned, as if something sinister
were about to unfold in the land of Krishna. 'Modi has
not taken the time to do something for the river Yamuna,'

he said. The real gau-rakshak is not happy. 'Yogi tries to be the thekedar of Hindus, but has only done lip service. Gau-raksha is only a political gimmick.' Sunil was unrelenting in his criticism. 'Nothing is happening on the ground.'

~

Somewhat like the way the Americans in Afghanistan distinguished between the good Taliban and the bad Taliban a decade ago, and were open to a dialogue with the good Taliban to restore peace in the region, Sunil has his own classification of Muslims, which reaffirms the general perception in this region. Almost 80 per cent of Muslims were once Hindus and converted to Islam a few hundred years ago. They are good Muslims, and there's a term for them in this region: Mev. They understand Hindu sentiments and respect them, and abstain from eating beef. They are even open to marrying their girls into Hindu families, said Sunil.

But having said that, Sunil explained what he believes are the basic differences between Hindus and Muslims. 'Hindus listen, they are submissive and amenable. Muslims are not. They are kattar (hardened), especially those who are not Mev. They are not concerned about the sentiments of Hindus when it comes to eating cows.'

Mev are very much part of the India story as Sunil sees it. They are patriots, their loyalty lies with India, and they still practice some Hindu traditions. In fact, he is working with them on issues pertaining to the restoration of the old glory of the region. 'Mev are very cooperative,' he emphasised.

It's the other category, the real Muslims, who are a problem, Sunil explained. And one out of every five Muslim families is linked with the leather trade. So their dependence on the cow is acute.

But it's also true that, of the six largest meat exporting companies in India, three are owned by Hindus.

Holy cow!

MEERUT

AN ENRICHING EXPERIENCE

We travelled extensively in the same region for over a year, meeting the people we introduced in this book. Some parts of the city of Meerut—a hotel, a dhaba, a bookshop—became very familiar. We found ourselves empathising with the people we spoke to, whether Sanauallah or Chetna Devi, despite their idiosyncrasies and views. We understood where their politics and world view came from. There are no extraordinary people, we learned. But for reasons beyond their comprehension or control, some people were confronted with extraordinary circumstances and surprised even themselves in the way they dealt with them.

Life manifests in paradoxes and ironies. People create complications in their lives and those of others, perhaps, in a search for meaning. They are victims of their own mindset, construing their biases as the word of God.

So far in this book, we have focused on specific people and events. In this last chapter, we present the isolated instances that enriched our journeys in and around the city of Meerut.

The Photographers' Hideout

A group of local news photographers meets every day in a little circular garden in the middle of a crossing close to the Meerut collectorate. They exchange information and pictures, plan their shoots and also where to meet for a cup of chai between assignments. News photography is a competitive profession, but news photographers have a strong sense of solidarity with each other. Those who congregate here are of all ages and descriptions, but they are a closely knit fraternity and speak a language of their own.

We spent many afternoons there while lining up our meetings. Raul was part of the gang. He had started his career here as a photographer for a Hindi daily about twenty years ago. He's younger than me, but a senior in the profession.

Food Is Fuel (And Delicious)

One of my favourite meals in Meerut was minced buff meat cooked on a thick hot plate on a slow flame for hours to make it as soft as butter. Strongly infused with spices and herbs, the aroma whets the appetite. It's best eaten with rumali roti. The taste lingers, allowing you to savour the meal long after the meal is done. If food is art, the Mughlai cuisine is a classical art form and traditional cooks are maestros.

You find this dish at a shack in the old city. It opens only after sundown and is run by two young Muslim men. Most of their customers are Hindus. The food is cheap: two people can feed themselves to a stupor for just a couple of hundred rupees. Follow this with a chai from the legendary tea shop at the Kotwali crossing. Raul loved the tea there, but it was too milky and sweet for my taste. At least once on each of our many trips to Meerut, we ate haleem and biryani at a place near Ghanta Ghar. It is the best haleem I have ever had.

The Printing Press

In Meerut, we often met some of Raul's friends in the backyard of a cluster of shops in the middle of the city. Abhishek, a local politician, is a retired soldier and now, a rich trader. He owns a printing press. In his early forties, he is a Hindu who married a Muslim woman. This was his second marriage and it didn't last long. In his own words, the marriage 'failed gloriously' and resulted in prolonged emotional consternation. He is a good businessman and has made a fortune, but has put on a lot of weight and suffers from ailments that are the outcome of unbridled consumption. His printing press is in the middle of the city, but hidden from view. His friends and the staff at his workshop are mostly Muslim. One of Abhishek's friends, Taufik, used to be a model. He runs a motor garage with his older brother.

A few local journalists meet at Abhishek's printing press and provide him with real news that may or may not be carried in the next day's newspapers. They sit together and get drunk, not every day but frequently. The party may continue late into the night. When we visited Meerut for our research, Mamu, to whom this book is dedicated, would stand beside his bike at one of these parties and sip tharra (country made liquor) from a plastic glass.

Each person at this frequent but impromptu party is acutely conscious of his own belief system, but nothing comes in the way of the bonhomie. Make no mistake: they are self-serving and a shade selfish and scheming. They have sometimes pushed one another the wrong way. But they continue to be good friends, open and tolerant of idiosyncrasies, views and beliefs. Arguments rarely happen, and when they do, no one takes them to heart. We spent many enjoyable evenings at the printing press.

Not Easy Being an Indian Muslim

One of the basic ideas of this book was that it needed to be experiential. We would not judge or cast aspersions on anyone, but we would also not shy away from writing about things as they were experienced. Many local journalists helped us, one of whom was a Muslim man we shall call Das Mohammad. This is not his real name.

Das Mohammad exemplifies the rift between the two biggest communities in India. The party now in power, as well as communal politics in general, have had a deep impact on the psyche of Muslims, because they have brainwashed many otherwise peace-loving Hindus.

On a good day, Das is a polite, resourceful and cooperative man. He has done well in his profession and knows all who matter in the region. He has friends in both the BJP and the Congress, though he resents being treated as a second-class citizen in his own motherland. But he treats this resentment like a hidden treasure. It is never spoken about.

As a journalist, he is skilled in the art of eliciting information for his stories, which are written tactfully so as not to earn the wrath of the people he has portrayed in a bad light. These stories are published in a leading Hindi daily. He is very helpful, and we were lucky to have him on our side.

Das has a certain way of functioning. He is not confrontational by nature, and keeps his yearnings to himself. An orphan, he is now married and a home-owner, and aspires to affluence and a better life. His career as a Muslim journalist is tricky, even difficult. He has to swallow insults against his faith with a smile on his face. Goons with political patronage have mercurial and violent temperaments, especially when it comes to matters concerning minorities. So far, Das has managed to evade their attention.

He accompanied us to some interviews and we had a meal at his home, which is located along a dusty highway where the noise of heavy vehicles drowns out the conversations.

Getting back from one of these trips late at night, past 10 p.m., Das was showing us a short cut to our destination. Raul was driving, and Das and I were sipping beer.

The detour took us on a narrow, muddy road. The night was pitch black and low-hanging dust made it worse. There was not a soul to be seen; it felt as though the area was under curfew. Das informed us that a certain stretch of this road was not safe. Cars are often stopped here and looted, he said. His anxiety filled the car, affecting us all.

Raul drove silently in the overwhelming darkness for half an hour and then took a sharp turn after negotiating a pothole. A tube light bisected the darkness before us. At that moment, I felt, for the first time, like a member of a minority. It was not a good feeling.

Das Mohammad took a deep breath and began babbling: 'Now, we are safe. We have crossed the notorious Jaat villages. Muslim villages start from here. They are not thugs, and I know a few people.' Clearly, notoriety and fair play are also identified by religion in this region. In his anxiety, Das had finished his bottle of beer very fast. He now wanted to share another with me. The alcohol chipped away at his usual prudence, giving way to plain talk and the inner resentment that had been concealed by his tact. It was an outburst and we were too tired to reason with him. So, he went on and on, until, at some point, a visibly embarrassed Raul asked him to change the subject. I was scribbling notes in my pad in the dark.

I don't remember what triggered this outrage. Perhaps, we had been discussing identities as a way to judge people— not just faith, but caste, creed, sexuality, everything! Even gender, a biological reality, is a potent identity employed to discriminate between fellow human beings.

Whatever triggered him, he got going. And there was no stopping him. 'Muslims are not treated well in this country, their own motherland. These Hindu miscreants are cowards. They are like serpents. They wouldn't dare venture out of their burrows if a person like the Mughal emperor Aurangzeb was ruling the country. They can only be tamed by the use of power. But the power is not with Muslims. When Muslims were in power, the Hindus were minnows. They should not forget the past. An insulted Muslim is a dangerous person. You cannot forever suppress a community. Fear for yourself; learn from history.' Das had a lot more to say, punctuated with a liberal use of derogatory words.

His outburst did not come from any place of power. Instead, he was like a mad man yelling in the street. This was an expression of desperation and helplessness, a reaction against being judged for his beliefs. I could only feel bad for him. Raul silently drove on.

The Little Girl and the Gita

Tall, thin ten-year-old Rida Zehra has been famous in Meerut for the last three years for a singular reason. Blind since birth, she is a Muslim who recites shlokas from the Gita with such flair and immaculate diction that even Brahmins, the traditional authorities on such texts, can't match her. She has won several competitions, acquiring appreciation and cash awards from sadhu-sant, or sages and saints, but continues to be a practising Muslim. She's blessed, people say. It's a gift from God, they all agree. Which God should get the credit for this though? Allah or Bhagwan?

Rida lives in the Brij Mohan School for the Blind in Meerut, where principal Praveen Sharma, his wife and their son Vibhav have been looking after the children in the school's care for the last ten years. The school decided to participate in a Gita-recitation competition on a whim. A few girls were taught shlokas and a select few participated in the competition. Rida stood first in her category. She had not been forced to learn the Gita. She was simply good at it.

The students at the school practice different shlokas from the Gita every day, and now, the girls can recite as many as three adhyay, or chapters, by heart. The Gita has eighteen chapters that contain seven hundred Sanskrit shlokas. The students have internalised them.

While many girls learn and recite shlokas from the Gita, Rida is perhaps the best and probably the only Muslim girl to do it. We met her one afternoon, but she was too shy to talk, merely nodding when we asked if she enjoyed reciting the shlokas. Some of the children were lying down in their dormitory, the curtains closed, the hum of the cooler lulling them to sleep. They were mostly under fourteen. The curtains had been pulled solely for privacy; light does not interfere in their daily lives.

A boy, about five years old, was sitting on a plastic chair beside the long table in the front veranda of the school. This space doubles as a classroom and a dining hall. He was waiting with two older children to be taken home. His face was blank, almost tranquil. I patted his head, but he betrayed no reaction. I imagined his heart beating inside his skinny frame. A child his age would be running around, but he sat there like a yogi. I spent a lot of time observing him while Raul took Rida's pictures. Blindness is a ticket to another world.

The Sharmas told us that many reporters, writers and photographers have come in the past, interacted with the children, taken pictures and never bothered to share a copy of the publication or the video with them. We promised to send them a copy of our book. Praveen Sharma gave us a list of gurus and sadhus who presented Rida with cash awards. These were passed on to her family. The blind school doesn't keep a penny of her winnings, he assured us. The care and upkeep of this school is not an easy task, but it is one to which he is clearly zealously devoted.

Sunil Singh in his room in Barsana, Mathura.

Hundreds of cows at the Gau Shala managed by Sunil Singh in Mathura.

The prostitutes of the Kabari Bazaar in Meerut collectively take care of Nihal, pay for his education, and want him to do well in life. His religion doesn't matter to them. This brothel is secular in the true sense of the word. Here, they believe in only one religion: humanity.

A woman stands tall in front of a policeman in Meerut.

Rida Zehra, a student at the Brij Mohan School for the Blind in Meerut, recites Bhagavad Gita from memory.

The irony was not lost on me. Meerut is the city of love jihad. It is also the city of Rida. I wondered: there is so much fanfare when a Muslim girl recites shlokas of the Gita with such facility. What if a Hindu girl mastered verses of the Quran and participated in a recitation competition? Would these people—the sages and saints—shower her with praise and money?

Soti Ganj

In the course of our long travels across western Uttar Pradesh, we discovered a discernible trend that must be properly researched. The older, more congested parts of any city, where tall houses are squeezed so close to each other that even sunlight is filtered many times before it falls on the damp streets, are increasingly becoming Muslim ghettos.

Mamu's brother-in-law runs an Urdu printing press from a house sold to him by a Hindu family in the neighbourhood of Zaidi Society. The Hindu family moved out because the neighbourhood had been overwhelmed by Muslims.

Soti Ganj in Meerut is an older neighbourhood where the Muslim population is significantly higher than other communities. It has the notorious distinction of being the chop shop hub of Meerut. Here, a perfectly functional car can be dismantled within an hour, and new cars can be reconstructed from the remains and with spare parts from other cars. Quite a feat!

Sixty-year-old Hafiz sahib lives in Soti Ganj, where he runs a two-generation-old car spares shop. He is a wise man, a repository of recent oral history, and spoke to us of communal clashes and riots in the past, and of the Hashimpura killings where justice delayed truly means justice denied. He was a young man when Hashimpura happened more than thirty years ago. Nineteen personnel of the Provincial Armed Constabulary (PAC) rounded up forty-two Muslim youths from Hashimpura in Meerut, shot them in cold blood and dumped their bodies in a nearby irrigation canal. The whole city went into shock and the secular credentials of the country were shaken to the core. Thirty years later, sixteen of those PAC men were convicted, but they were only lower-level functionaries— those who carried out the orders. The 'mastermind' was never held responsible, never investigated despite a mention of his purported role in the case diaries that formed the basis of investigations.

Hafiz sahib compared this past with the present. 'The situation is even worse today because the state overtly favours one community over the other,' he said in Urdu. When two strong communities coexist, there is bonhomie. But there will be clashes as well. 'Even brothers fight,' he said. 'There's nothing unusual about that.'

He halted to collect his thoughts and was distressed to say what he was about to articulate. 'Never has the situation been so bad,' he said. 'Muslims don't just feel targeted by another community, but also by another faith; belligerent believers of a religion that outnumber their own. But there's something much graver. They feel they are being targeted by the state. The protector has joined hands with the aggressor. There is no fair play. No one feels safe.'

But not all is lost, he added. He has faith in the idea of India that is enshrined in the Constitution; the idea of unity in diversity and not uniformity by coercion. 'This is a phase in the history of a great nation, my motherland. It will pass. Like good times, bad times are also transitory.' He spoke in Urdu with poetic grace. I was filled with a sense of sadness. The clashes can't go on forever because the two communities are interlinked and interdependent in the socio-economic life of Meerut, a fact that is true for the rest of the region and the rest of the country.

The Sahar Kazi

Zaimus Sajidai is the sahar kazi (chief priest of district) who solemnised the marriage of Shallu and Kalim. He lives in Kahir Nagar, an old, congested part of Meerut. He studied religion in Deoband and graduated from Aligarh Muslim University, where he now teaches Muslim theology. Approaching his sixties, he's soft-spoken and wide-viewed. He does not speak with bitterness about the current communal situation, but doesn't shun frankness for politeness. He was seated in a narrow rectangular room crammed with oversized sofas placed along the walls on either side, with a small window opening into a narrow, noisy street, curtains closed.

Meerut is a city of 'mushtanka tahzeeb' or composite culture, where Hindus and Muslims have lived in peace for centuries. 'The popular belief still is that the secular credentials of the city are preserved,' he told us, emphasising the word 'still'.

We talked about the ghettoisation of Muslim populations in Indian cities, not just in Meerut. This indicates that the community as a whole is entering a shell and becoming alienated from the mainstream. People feel safe in these little hideouts, we suggested.

Sahar Kazi did not agree. 'This is a false impression. All festivals are celebrated here—Diwali and Eid—with equal gaiety,' he said.

But there's no denying the fact that the BJP–RSS agenda has created a rift between the communities and there is a crisis of trust at this time. 'They are slowly and progressively succeeding,' he said, regretfully.

Like Hafiz sahib, Sahar Kazi also looked to the past to explain the situation today. Speaking in Hindustani, he pointed out that communal clashes are not new. When communities and faith live together, people fight and also fall in love. Meerut has witnessed many communal clashes in the past, but those were about petty local issues. Today, clashes happen in an organised manner, with the media fanning the communal flames. Faith has become integral to politics, but religion shouldn't be the basis on which to fight elections, he said. All minorities, not just Muslims, are bound to be anxious about this.

'I have attended many RSS public programmes,' he said to clarify that his criticism is informed, and added, '*Fistafarasti ka zahar poore desh mai phail gaya hai* (the poison of divisive politics has spread through the entire country).'

Falling in love is such a natural thing, he said. 'Love is spontaneous; it cannot be part of some sinister plan or conspiracy.' Love cannot be a political issue either. 'They call it "love jihad",' he said. 'Such a ridiculous term.' No one knows what jihad really means. In popular parlance, jihad is a synonym for terrorism or a religious war, but the Quran sets out three kinds of jihad.

Jihad is a struggle, he explained. The first and foremost jihad is with the self, 'to improve yourself and to improve all of humanity'. The second jihad is the jihad against Satan, who misleads people and promotes fear and hatred. Satan can be contained by preaching and propagating the word of God through dialogue and other peaceful means. And, Sahar Kazi asserted, 'A true Muslim would never advocate violence and coercion to spread Islam.'

The third kind of jihad is against an 'open enemy', which is not the BJP government or the RSS or fellow human beings. An open enemy, according to the Quran, is defined by situations meeting one of these five conditions: the need for self-defence; when persecuted for their faith; to preserve peace; when their lives are threatened for following their faith; and last but not the least, to protect universal religious freedom. Sahar Kazi spoke with clarity. He seemed like a lamp of reason in the engulfing darkness caused by the pettiness of religious politics.

Recollecting his interaction with Shallu and Kalim, he explained that, while Shallu's family had not been happy with the choices she made, they were not militantly against them either. They would have given their blessings after some resistance. But when the matter was blown out of proportion, and politicians and police came into the picture, her family found themselves under tremendous pressure. 'The police pressured her but she didn't relent. That's the power of love,' he said.

He agreed that marrying into the Muslim community is tricky compared to other faiths. 'The partner has to convert to Islam or the marriage is not valid,' he said. Raul pointed out that this restriction is not applicable when Christians marry into Islam, for they have the same prophets and are considered people of the book.

All said and done, however, who to marry is a personal choice. The Special Marriage Act ensures that considerations of faith don't come in the way of any matrimonial union. 'No one is concerned about people, it's all about the votes,' Sahar Kazi added.

But introspection is also necessary. 'You cannot entirely blame others for your miseries,' he said, acknowledging the growing radicalisation of his own community. There used to be no restriction on teaching science and mathematics in any madrassa. 'The basic difference between being taught in a madrassa and in a university is that, in the former case, people tend to get judgemental, and there are hardly any career options available apart from propagating your faith,' Sahar Kazi said. The madrassa is also moving towards radicalisation. However, he added, the madrassas did not advocate the partition of India. 'Madrassas were pro-independence and opposed to the Partition of 1947,' he said. 'They participated in the freedom struggle for the love of the nation.' Raising his voice, Sahar Kazi said firmly, 'If a Muslim follows his religion in its true spirit, it is in no way anti-Hindu.'

Sadia, the Lawyer

Though we made Meerut our base of operations, we often visited neighbouring cities. Muzaffarnagar is just an hour's drive from Meerut and we spent a lot of time at the local court there, collecting documents. In Muzaffarnagar, we met some of the lawyers representing Muslim families who've been wrongly implicated in malicious cases. There are many Shallus in the region, so many that some Muslim lawyers have made it a point to not represent Hindus. This is not because they will never run out of cases representing Muslims, but a reaction to the many, many instances of discrimination against Muslims. They hold the whole majority community responsible for electing the BJP to power which the western media refers to as the 'Hindu nationalist party.' I argued that, by boycotting a community from representation in court, they are not uplifting their own community; rather, they are perpetuating the very idea that they feel victimised by in the first place. They offered us the sweet, milky tea that is typical of this region. It's a little like hot sugar syrup that vaguely smells like tea.

In the old city of Muzaffarnagar, a communally sensitive locality with dense housing lined along the maze of dirty lanes and bylanes, lives Sadia. Her Muslim-dominated locality, Mirza Nagar, has a rather notorious reputation.

Sadia was Sarita before she married Mohammad Umar five years ago. They are both advocates. She has been dubbed a victim of love jihad, but she considers herself the winner, and master of her own destiny. It was not easy—a lot was at stake. But once she made up her mind, there was no going back.

'This marriage is the best thing that has happened to me,' she told us happily.

Sadia's new Muslim family is very supportive of her career and her success. Recently, she was elected representative of Ward 46 in the local municipal council.

Now in her late twenties, she's expecting her second child and is also preparing for the civil services and judicial services examinations. She wants to be either a cop or a judge—she wants to dispense justice. Her head is covered, but her voice is loud and clear, and has gravitas. Having got through her tumultuous past, she is confident about her future.

When Sadia, who as Sarita belonged to a sub-caste called Bajada Gotra and lived in a town called Khatoli, three hours from Muzaffarnagar, told her family that she was marrying a Muslim man, she faced much opposition. But she went ahead and married the man she loved. When her family learned that she had married Mohammad Umar, they disowned her.

At least, her family didn't try to kill her. And, unlike Shallu, Sadia didn't get caught in a political hailstorm. All she faced was her family's contempt, though that was bad enough. When they disowned her, she felt a part of her body had been cut off. She was an emotional wreck when she began living with her husband.

But his family welcomed her and accepted her as one of their own. Sadia started to rebuild her life bit by bit. She didn't just adopt a new family, but also a new way of life. In the past five years, no one from her family has come to see her. One of her brothers, however, was kind enough to come and hand over her papers, certificates and degree so she could resume her studies.

We met Sadia and her family late one evening after a long drive from Meerut. It was already dark and the street looked deserted except for a cow listlessly munching garbage in the middle of the road. We were welcome guests, thanks to being accompanied by a local reporter who knew the family well.

Sadia's is a joint family of lawyers that lives in a big double-storied house with a covered terrace. We sat in their study, which doubles as a drawing room. The wall on the far side was covered from floor to ceiling with bookshelves. Dusty law journals were stashed on them. Near the table was a sofa set with soiled floral-print upholstery. We were treated to snacks over two rounds of tea. Curious neighbours dropped by, but were asked to return later.

Their house is much bigger than one would anticipate in this congested locality with scraggy roads. And her family fully understands—or tries to understand—the situation from Sadia's standpoint. They are aware of how she feels about being cut off from her past. They try to empower her. Their love has filled the void within her.

Sadia was the last to arrive at the table. I felt that they were hesitant to let strangers meet the woman of the house. The mother of a three-year-old boy, she was pregnant and arrived with her face covered with a red scarf. She hesitated to speak with us at first, but soon, opened up. Sadia is slender and tall, resolute in her ideas and her ambitions. The fact that she is ambitious is celebrated in her husband's family.

She has created a niche for herself. After she married, she did a degree in law, followed by a master's degree in political science. Her new family is confident that she will achieve much more in life; that her victory in the local municipal elections is just a beginning.

Sadia spoke at length about communal politics and how her in-laws understood very well the larger political dynamics of it. An inter-faith marriage might have further repercussions too. Sadia could spell trouble for the whole family. But they are supportive. They will protect her, she said. She feels safe here. And her in-laws are not bitter about her family's attitude towards Muslims. They seem to understand where this hate comes from and will welcome them if they wish to resume contact with their daughter.

It was nice to be with them. For a change, I liked the sweet tea. The state and their agents have no business disturbing the tranquillity of Sadia's home, a heartening example of India's composite culture.

Secularism in a Brothel

The most secular of all the places we visited was Meerut's red-light area, Kabari Bazaar. Here, people deal with each other without considerations of faith, caste or creed. It's a secretive world of hidden activities, where anonymity allows people to do things they would kill others for doing in public life. The secrecy allows them to unleash their untempered selves, and the picture—thus revealed—is not pretty. Any red-light area is an exploitative set-up that caters to a hypocritical society. Meerut's Kabari Bazaar is no exception.

When people enter this hidden world and unleash their true selves, they are highly exploitative, carnal, racist (fair girls are priced higher) and abusive. But, ironically, not communal. Caste, creed and religion are relegated to the margins. They become monsters all right, in this secure, hidden space, but never communal. I emphasise this fact because it indicates that communalism and casteist pettiness is not in our inherent nature. It is a socio-political construct that we are expected to adhere to. Politicians provoke communal sentiments for votes and to hide their failings. Even the most ardent supporters of identity-based discrimination become very secular in this space. I can tell you several stories to substantiate this revelation, but one stands out. Shilpa was a Hindu girl forced into prostitution in 2010, 'due to circumstances beyond her control'. In other words, her family was desperately poor. She was so young and beautiful that the pimps considered her 'export quality' and sent her to Saudi Arabia in 2011. She lived there for a year, meeting clients at five-star hotels.

According to the traditional Islamic jurisprudence, sex without the purpose of reproduction is unlawful or zinā. Prostitution falls in the category of zinā, as do adultery, fornication, rape, sodomy, incest, bestiality and homosexuality. All these are hadd, or crimes that have specified punishments in the Quran.

Shilpa met a certain sheikh more than once, and when she became pregnant by him, she decided to keep the child, return to India and resume her life in Kabari Bazaar.

Her son was born in Meerut and named 'Nihal' after the hotel where he was conceived. In 2018, Shilpa died of AIDS. Nihal was not even seven years old. He is now the son of every prostitute in Kabari Bazaar. They pool their resources to ensure that he gets a good education at an English-medium school. They want him to be a good human being.

One of the people I met on this trip and have deep admiration for is Dr Atul Sharma. A social activist in her fifties, she works for the dignity of the sex workers in Kabari Bazaar and ensures that they receive regular medical help. She is also the mother of three grown-up children, a daughter and two sons, who are well-settled in life.

She was seated in a big revolving chair crammed behind a big table in a small room. Her office resembles that of a deputy collector except for its size. She speaks with bureaucratic arrogance and her opinion of journalists is not very encouraging. Given the way the media behaved in the love jihad case, this is understandable.

Dr Sharma described herself as a feminist and explained what it means. 'Women should be masters of their destiny, which also means they are free to make mistakes,' she said. 'This is what I tell my daughter.' Gender played no role in the way she brought up her children. 'Girls should not get special treatment, sympathies or concessions,' she asserted. 'But it also has to be ensured that they are not at a disadvantage because they are women.'

Dr Sharma feels—and we agree—that love jihad is a political controversy and nothing deeper. It was just a way to create a rift between the two biggest communities in the country. She had met Shallu's and Kalim's families and had participated in many of Shallu's court hearings. She admires Shallu and calls her 'the master of her destiny'. After all, the young woman is from one of the most patriarchal castes in the local Hindu society, which she describes as 'Marshal Kaum', namely Tyagi, Jaats, Gujjars and Thakurs, who are known to be strict about sticking to the community's rules. Any deviation from the norm calls for violent retribution, even death. In this context, such a thing as love jihad, Dr Sharma pointed out, 'cannot be tolerated'.

Western Uttar Pradesh and the state of Haryana report the maximum honour killings in the country.

Khap panchayats—an assembly of village elders who are the custodians of age-old customs and traditions—are quasi-judicial bodies that liberally award death sentences to young couples who have eloped or have had an inter-caste or inter-faith marriage. Dr Sharma was very matter-of-fact about Shallu's case. 'Her own family threatened to kill her. The whole country seemed against their love story. Like it or not, Kalim's family accepted Shallu unconditionally, despite the fact that all hell had broken loose. Shallu's family toed the line that the politicians set. She was betrayed by her own family. They supported the political narrative against their own daughter. The support they were offered by politicians was like a disguise for bribes. V.K. Singh, the former chief of the army, now a BJP minister, called on her family to affirm his support against their own daughter.'

As far as Dr Sharma is concerned, Shallu, the master of her own destiny, is the poster girl of feminism.

ACKNOWLEDGEMENTS

The Srivastava family: Sushma, Mudit–Ranajan, Mayank–Ruchi, Madhulika–Alok, Yash–Neha, Shradha–Divyanshu, Srishti, Kshitij and Avantika.

The Irani family: Sagheer, Shaheen, Aayesha, Romaan, Gulnaar, Arhaan.

Shashank Bhagat and Reshma Bhagat for their tacit support.

The Patriot newspaper and *Open* magazine.

Karthika V.K. for reaffirming our faith in our profession by encouraging this journalistic endeavour.

A NOTE ON THE COVER

During namaz, one performs the gesture where the index finger is pointed in the direction of Kaaba and recites 'Ashadu an la ilaha illa'llah wa Ashad anna Muhammadan Rasululullah' to reaffirm faith in the one God—the only one, 'Allah'. And, to testify that Muhammad is the messenger of God.

While making that gesture, in the image, there is a woman holding a trishula or trident. The trident signifies that Shiva—the enlightened one—is beyond these three gunas or tendencies namely, rajas (passion), tamas (darkness, destructive) and sattva (purity), and the one who holds the three lokas namely, swarga (heaven), bhu (earth) and patala (netherworld) together. This is one of the many interpretations.

The trident and the finger together resemble 'Allah' in the Arabic script. The image signifies unity in diversity—religion, languages, caste and creed—that's our greatest asset, our national identity. There are many paths to attain the sacred goal. And that, 'we are different' is a reason to celebrate not to fight.